W9-BLF-972

HEALTHY EATING

A Guide to Nutrition

Nutrition and Food Safety

HEALTHY EATING: A GUIDE TO NUTRITION

HEALTHY EATING

A Guide to Nutrition

Nutrition and Food Safety

Terry L. Smith

CHELSEA HOUSE
PUBLISHERS
An imprint of Infobase Publishing

NUTRITION AND FOOD SAFETY

Chelsea House
An imprint of Infobase Publishing
132 West 31st Street
New York, NY 10001

Library of Congress Cataloging-in-Publication Data

Smith, Terry L.
  Nutrition and food safety / Terry L. Smith.
    p. cm. — (Healthy eating: a guide to nutrition)
  Includes bibliographical references and index.
  ISBN 978-1-60413-776-7 (hardcover)
  1. Food—Safety measures—Popular works. 2. Nutrition—Popular works.
3. Foodborne diseases—Popular works. I. Title. II. Series.
  RA601.S65 2011
  363.19′2—dc22

2010021324

Text design by Annie O'Donnell
Cover design by Alicia Post
Illustrations by Sholto Ainslie for Infobase Publishing
Composition by Mary Susan Ryan Flynn
Cover printed by Bang Printing, Brainerd, Minn.
Book printed and bound by Bang Printing, Brainerd, Minn.
Date printed: November 2010
Printed in the United States of America

10 9 8 7 6 5 4 3 2 1

This book is printed on acid-free paper.

CONTENTS

INTRODUCTION

A hundred years ago, people received nutritional guidance from mothers and grandmothers: Eat your carrots because they're good for your eyes; don't eat too many potatoes because they'll make you fat; be sure to get plenty of roughage so you can more easily move your bowels. Today, everyone seems to offer more advice: Take a vitamin supplement to optimize your health; don't eat fish with cabbage because you won't be able to digest them together; you can't stay healthy on a vegetarian diet. Nutrition is one of those topics about which all people seem to think they know something, or at least have an opinion. Whether it is the clerk in your local health food store recommending that you buy supplements or the woman behind you in line at the grocery store raving about the latest low-carbohydrate diet, everyone is ready to offer you nutritional advice. How do you know what to believe or, more importantly, what to do?

The purpose of these books is to help you answer these questions. Even if you don't love learning about science, at the very least you probably enjoy certain foods and want to stay healthy—or become healthier. In response to this, these books are designed to make the science you *need* to understand as palatable as the foods you love. Once you understand the basics, you can apply this simple health knowledge to your everyday decisions about nutrition and health. The **Healthy Eating** set includes one book with all of the basic nutrition information you need to choose a healthy diet, as well as five others that cover topics of special concern to many: weight management, exercise, disease prevention, food safety, and eating disorders.

Our goal is not to tell you to stop eating potato chips and candy bars, give up fast food, or always eat your vegetables. Instead, it is to provide you with the information you need to make informed choices about your diet. We hope you will recognize that potato chips and candy are not poison, but they should only be eaten as occasional treats. We hope you will decide for yourself that fast food is something you can indulge in every now and then, but is not a good choice every day. We encourage you to recognize that although you should eat your vegetables, not everyone always does, so you should do your best to try new vegetables and fruits and eat them as often as possible.

These books take the science of nutrition out of the classroom and allow you to apply this information to the choices you make about foods, exercise, dietary supplements, and other lifestyle decisions that are important to your health. This knowledge should help you choose a healthy diet while allowing you to enjoy the diversity of flavors, textures, and tastes that food provides, and also encouraging you to explore the meanings food holds in our society. When you eat a healthy diet, you will feel good in the short term and enjoy health benefits in the long term. We can't personally evaluate each meal you consume, but we believe these books will give you the tools to make your own nutritious choices.

Lori A. Smolin, Ph.D., and
Mary B. Grosvenor, M.S., R.D.

1

INTRODUCTION TO FOOD SAFETY

Food safety was far from dance instructor Stephanie Smith's mind as she enjoyed the hamburger her mother prepared for dinner one fall Sunday in 2007. Yet over the next few days, Smith developed gradually worsening symptoms of an intestinal illness. Five days after eating the hamburger, Smith became so incapacitated by pain that she was admitted to the hospital. Doctors had to put her in a coma for nine weeks to control her seizures. She survived, but the illness left her with severely damaged kidneys and unable to walk. As reported in a 2009 *New York Times* article, Smith continues to ask herself, "Why me?" and "Why from a hamburger?"

Smith had the great misfortune to eat a hamburger that had been contaminated with an especially virulent strain of *Escherichia coli*, identified scientifically as **O157:H7**, based on certain distinctive markers. Health officials estimate that tens of thousands of people are sickened by *E. coli* O157:H7 each year. A small percentage of them develop a serious condition called *hemolytic*

FIGURE 1.1 Former children's dance instructor Stephanie Smith became severely ill with an *E. coli* infection from tainted hamburger meat and, as a result, is now paralyzed.

uremic syndrome, and a few have even more severe outcomes such as Smith's. Most *E. coli* O157:H7 **contamination** occurs in ground beef, even though it has been illegal for companies and grocers to sell ground beef contaminated with this virulent strain since an outbreak in 2004 caused the deaths of four children. *E. coli* O157:H7 contamination has also been detected in other foods, such as fruit juice and lettuce.

The contaminated hamburger Smith ate that Sunday was sold by Cargill, an international producer and marketer of food products. However, Cargill did not produce the beef from which the frozen patties were made. Rather, the patties were prepared from meat products obtained from at least three **slaughterhouses** and from a company that processes fatty trimmings carved from better cuts of meat. By using these combined sources, Cargill was able to reduce their costs by about 25% from the cost of making hamburger patties from a single meat source. Some of the low-grade meat products used in the manufacture of hamburger patties come from parts of a cow that are more likely to be contaminated with **feces**, and, thus, are more likely to harbor *E. coli* O157:H7. Cargill did not test the various meats and trimmings for contamination before mixing them to make hamburger patties. Thus, it was impossible for federal investigators to pinpoint the original source of the bacteria that sickened Smith and others.

Continuing outbreaks of *E. coli* O157:H7 contamination have increased pressure on the U.S. Department of Agriculture and on the meatpacking industry to improve the safety of our food supply. Additional guidelines for industry procedures and food inspections have been imposed, but food safety experts contend that much more is required to assure that food supplies are free of the contamination that had such a devastating effect on Stephanie Smith's life.

HISTORY OF FOOD SAFETY

It is likely that the first prehistoric people to enjoy a meal of roasted meat were delighted at how much better it tasted compared to raw foods. Little did they know that their discovery of fire for cooking their food was also the first step toward reducing foodborne illnesses. Although history does not record the details, it is certain that people have suffered and died from foodborne illness beginning with the very origins of man. Ancient people roamed their surroundings in search of edible plants and animals, and it is logical to assume they would have most easily captured animals that were sickly and more likely to harbor disease. Because people lacked methods for preserving food, they no doubt ate spoiled and rancid foods that made them sick. Plus, many of them probably died from eating poisonous mushrooms and other toxic plants before they learned which ones to avoid.

Gradually, primitive people shifted to a system of farming and domestication of animals. Methods of food preservation were

(continues on page 14)

ERGOTISM: THE "CEREAL" KILLER

The Middle Ages in Europe were dark times of poverty, violence, disease, and ignorance. They lasted for a thousand years, from the fifth to the fifteenth centuries. A sense of fear hung over the gloom,

FIGURE 1.2 Some people see the signs of humans suffering from disease in Hieronymus Bosch's painting *The Temptation of St. Anthony*, created circa 1500.

and misfortunes of all kinds were blamed on demons. Though poor people were at the mercy of cruel kings, marauding soldiers, and greedy neighbors, what killed many of them was the coarse rye bread that was their main food source. Ergotism, the disease caused by the toxic fungus that grows on grain crops, was a horrible way to die. The fungus most often grew on rye, a cereal grain that served as the common food of poor people in the Middle Ages. An early name for the disease was Holy Fire, after the tremendous burning sensations in the arms and legs as the toxins cut off circulation. When the fungus was baked into bread, it produced an LSD-like substance that caused victims to hallucinate. (One can only imagine the tormented visions they suffered.) An order of monks built hospitals that provided care for the victims of ergotism. The monks dedicated their works to St. Anthony, and eventually the disease was given the name St. Anthony's Fire.

The suffering of disease victims inspired artists of the times. For example, modern museum goers are fascinated by the paintings of Hieronymus Bosch (c. 1450–1516). Bosch filled his canvases with fanciful creatures, deformed monsters, and scary demons. Bosch lived near the end of the Middle Ages and was familiar with the folklore and superstitions of the times. He also would have known about diseases such as St. Anthony's Fire. He was a religious man, and many of his paintings portrayed religious themes. One of his most famous paintings, *The Temptation for Saint Anthony*, portrays the life of this celebrated saint. Yet this painting obviously does much more than tell a religious story. It shows a weird landscape populated by fanciful animals, odd objects, and strange people. It is a fascinating challenge to study this painting to try to understand its symbolism—is Bosch perhaps trying to portray his vision of hell?

(continued from page 11)

discovered, such as drying, salting, and fermentation. Still, early recorded history includes references to dietary practices and records of mass deaths that suggest the existence of foodborne illness. Some scientists have interpreted the biblical story of a severe plague following an Israelite feast of quail as a case of mass food poisoning.

Outbreaks of one particularly strange foodborne disease were familiar to Europeans of the Middle Ages. It was commonly called Holy Fire. Many believed that the horrible suffering people endured from the disease was a punishment from God. Victims' bodies might be twisted in pain while their arms and legs felt like they were on fire. In the 1600s, a French physician noted that the timing of these **outbreaks** corresponded to grain harvests in which strange growths appeared on some of the grains. Eventually, the physician's observations were proved correct, and the disease was named ergotism. It is caused by *ergot*, a toxic fungus that grows on grain crops and ultimately ends up being baked into the bread made from the grain. It is even possible that the hallucinations experienced by the accusers of the Salem Witch Trial may have been due to the same toxins in bread that came from the local bakery.

One modern reading of Bosch's St. Anthony painting suggests that it is symbolically portraying the effects of a terrible real-life disease. Perhaps the strange animals are the wild hallucinations of someone suffering from ergotism. A fire in the background suggests the disease's terrible burning sensations and the disease's common name of St. Anthony's Fire. An amputated foot may represent the loss of limbs. One vegetable-shaped creature may represent a plant that was commonly used to ease the pain of sufferers. An odd building is shaped like equipment that was used by druggists at the time. It may be that Bosch was, in his own unique way, showing us not only the facts of the disease but what it meant in terms of human suffering.

The horrors of war have been made even more horrific by the presence of foodborne illnesses on the battlefield. Almost every war through history has an accompanying story of soldiers dying from disease rather than in actual battle. In the fifth century B.C., the Plague of Athens, which hastened the end of the Golden Age of Greece through its defeat by Sparta, was likely caused by a food borne illness. Lead poisoning of wine may have contributed to the fall of the Roman Empire. Many more soldiers in the Spanish-American War died of disease than in battle. (Typhoid fever spread by the unsanitary conditions of the training camps was the biggest killer.) The nineteenth-century Opium Wars between Britain and China even featured a case of intentional poisoning. It seems a clever Chinese baker noted that the occupying British ate bread while the local people ate rice. He hatched a scheme to add arsenic to the bread, sold in a bakery frequented by the foreigners. Fortunately, the scheme was detected, and very few actually died from the poison.

Overview of Food Production

Colonial America was a farming society. As of 1776, 90% of Americans were farmers. Today, less than 1% of Americans claim farming as their occupation. The colonists had only primitive transportation systems, so there was no question of shipping food over long distances. Today, food arrives at our grocery stores from all over the United States and many foreign countries. Early farmers practiced crop rotation to improve their soil and control pests. Modern farmers rely on chemical fertilizers and pesticides.

The hard-working immigrants who settled the plains of America in the 1800s were delighted with the productive agricultural land they found there. They established small, close-knit farming communities where neighbors helped each other build their barns and plant and harvest their crops each year. Meanwhile, other immigrants were drawn to the growing American cities to work in the great factories of the Industrial Revolution. Mechanization in the form of farm machinery led to greater efficiency of food production. Because of this, the size of the average farm grew larger, as the new machinery allowed a single family to farm more acreage. Improved transportation meant that grains

FIGURE 1.3 Crop rotation is a central element of early farming. Here, teams of oxen and horses aid in clearing farmland for spring planting in the 1800s.

and farm animals could be shipped long distances to provide the growing city populations with food. New methods of food preservation, processing, and storage were invented to deal with the increasing complexity of the food distribution system. Over time, America changed from a rural economy to an urban economy that depended on fewer and fewer farmers to provide food.

Our food production system today can be more accurately described as an industry, with agriculture playing a relatively small role. Only about 20 cents of every food dollar goes to the farmers and ranchers who produce the food. The rest goes to industries that are responsible for processing, distributing, and marketing our foods. Farms often consist of large commercial tracts that grow only a single crop. Such monoculture systems encourage the development of crop-specific pests, which necessitates the use of chemical pesticides. A pig that is destined to become bacon on American breakfast tables spends its entire short life in a confined pen, packed in so tightly that its tail is clipped to prevent it from being bitten off by other pigs. Doses of **antibiotics** are routinely administered to food animals to prevent the spread of diseases that are much more likely to occur in such tight quarters. Dairy cows receive **hormones** in order to increase their milk production. The industries that provide agricultural chemicals, seed, and antibiotics play an essential and powerful role in our food system.

The food processing industry employs thousands of people and consists of diverse and widespread manufacturing plants. These plants process meats, agricultural products, and chemicals to produce the frozen pizzas and countless other food items that we purchase at our grocery stores. And how do all these food items end up on our grocery shelves? Stocking those shelves requires a complex system of wholesalers, refrigerated storage units, and shipping facilities that can respond quickly to seasonal food variations and consumer demands. Finally, there are the countless business outlets where we purchase our foods, from the corner coffee stand to the mega-grocery store.

Developing Food Safety Measures

Over time, as the food supply was transferred more and more from local farm families into the hands of food producers and merchants, more opportunities for accidental or intentional contamination arose. In nineteenth-century England, beer, wine, bread, and other foods were routinely **adulterated** with cheaper ingredients by their makers. Usually, the intent was merely to substitute a cheaper product so the merchant could make a bigger profit, but some of the substituted ingredients

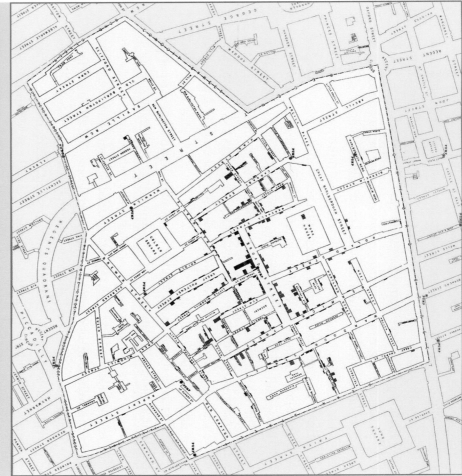

FIGURE 1.4 This map, made in 1854 by Dr. John Snow, highlights deaths from cholera (each one represented by a black dash) and nearby water pumps, which were suspected to be contaminated, in a London neighborhood.

had unhealthy side effects. Dairy cows that provided milk for the early residents of New York City were fed such a meager diet that their milk took on a bluish color, and it was delivered to local neighborhoods by the same trucks that carted away the cow manure. People began to give more thought to their food purchases and demanded action from public officials to assure the safety and purity of their food.

Advances in science during the 1800s and early 1900s awoke people to the fact that many of the illnesses from which they suffered could be traced to their food and drink. John Snow, a London physician, became suspicious when he noted that patients who were suffering from an 1854 cholera outbreak were concentrated in a single neighborhood. He drew up elaborate maps showing exactly where they lived and eventually traced the cause of the outbreak to water from a single contaminated well that supplied all of their houses. Snow's investigation is regarded as the beginning of **epidemiology**, the study of the factors that cause illnesses in populations. Years later, scientists working in the new field of microbiology identified the organism that caused cholera, along with causative agents for other waterborne and foodborne illnesses.

From 1902 to 1907, the attention of the American public was riveted on the eating habits of 12 young men who came to be known as the "Poison Squad." A popular song was even written about them and what they ate. These young men volunteered to eat their meals in the basement of the U.S. government's Bureau of Chemistry in Washington, D.C. Scientists observed the men for changes in their health and digestion after they dined on meals spiked with various **food additives**. The experiments were authorized by Congress and duly reported in newspapers and scientific publications of the day. While some might question the scientific value of these early experiments in food safety, there is no question about their impact on the American public. This period also saw the publication of *The Jungle*, Upton Sinclair's famous novel that exposed the horrible unsanitary conditions within the Chicago meatpacking industry. The resulting clamor from the public finally resulted in passage of the Pure Food and Drug Act of 1906, the first major U.S. regulation of the food industry, and a companion act, the Meat Inspection Act. These acts did much more than impose regulations on food. They also changed the mind-set of the country about the responsibility of government to keep our food safe and set in motion a public interest in the issue that continues to this day.

(continues on page 22)

TYPHOID MARY:
AN INNOCENT CARRIER OF DISEASE?

When Irish immigrant Mary Mallon first encountered the public health system of New York City, she greeted a visiting health official with harsh words and a meat fork in her hand. One can only wonder what this hard-working woman understood of the official's accusations that she had caused the illness of dozens of people. Mallon had immigrated to the United States as a teenager and worked her way up to the desirable position of household cook for several prominent families. By her own account, she had never been sick a day in her life, so the suggestion that she had passed on a serious disease to others must have seemed outlandish to her. Yet the historical facts indicate that she was indeed a silent **carrier** of the bacteria that cause typhoid, and that the disease was accidentally spread to household members by bacteria passed from her feces and, by way of her hands, into meals that she prepared.

Typhoid fever is a life-threatening, foodborne illness caused by bacteria of the *Salmonella* family—*Salmonella typhi*—that grow in the

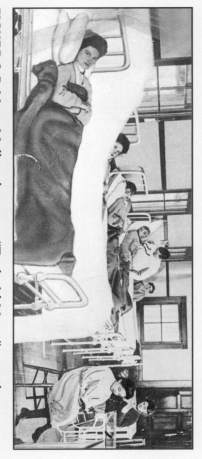

FIGURE 1.5 Mary Mallon, know as "Typhoid Mary," was the first person identified as a healthy carrier of typhoid bacilli in the United States. She is pictured here while institutionalized on Brother Island, where she stayed from 1915 until her death in 1938.

intestinal tract of an infected individual and are shed through the feces. Typhoid outbreaks had been occurring throughout the centuries, but it was not until the 1880s that the causative agent was identified. Soon thereafter, public health departments opened in major cities, and they were determined to use new scientific information to wipe out typhoid and other infectious diseases. Officials were given broad powers to investigate disease outbreaks and to **quarantine** infected individuals. This period happened to coincide with a large wave of immigrants coming to the United States. There was considerable prejudice against foreigners, many of whom were poor and forced to live in crowded, unsanitary conditions. The stage was set for finding unsuspecting immigrants on whom officials could lay the blame for disease outbreaks.

In the summer of 1906, several cases of typhoid broke out in the household of a wealthy family vacationing on Long Island. After lengthy investigation, suspicion focused on the cook who left her position about the time of the outbreak, Mary Mallon. The unwary woman was soon tracked down, leading to the meat fork encounter with the health official. Eventually, Mallon was taken into custody. Her feces samples indicated she was, indeed, a carrier of the typhoid bacteria. She had evidently experienced such a mild case of typhoid that it went unrecognized, but she was unlucky to be among the small percentage of typhoid victims who continue to harbor the bacteria in their intestines. Despite her good health, Mary was quarantined by the health department and became the subject of a banner headline in a sensationalist newspaper of the day: "'Typhoid Mary' Most Harmless and Yet the Most Dangerous Woman in America." After three years, Mary was released from quarantine but was returned when found to be working once again as a cook. She died after spending 26 years in captivity, at the age of 69.

(continued from page 19)

REGULATION OF FOOD SAFETY
Food and Drug Administration

The Food and Drug Administration (FDA) was initiated in 1906 when Congress passed the Food and Drug Act and charged the agency with prohibiting the interstate transport of adulterated or mislabeled foods or drugs. Chemists and inspectors were hired, and they set about the task of protecting the public from the unhealthy practices of the food industry. However, they soon ran up against a problem that continues to this day: The food and beverage industries are huge and politically powerful, and they fought back against regulation by this upstart agency. A controversial addition to the FDA's authority was nicknamed the "Delaney clause." The law established a "zero tolerance" policy for any additive or pesticide residue in processed food that was found to cause cancer. Consumer groups opposed the Delaney clause, claiming it did not protect the public because of the many loopholes that the clause contained. The agriculture industry opposed it because it barred the use of possibly safe pesticides. The fight raged on for years in Congress and in the courts. Finally, Congress passed reform legislation for food safety in 1996. The Delaney clause was gone but in its place came powerful new protections for consumers.

Today's FDA is one of the United States's largest government agencies. It is responsible for promoting health by reviewing research and approving new products, ensuring that our foods are safe and properly labeled, and working with consumer groups and scientific experts. As part of the Department of Health and Human Services, the agency works closely with Congress, many other federal agencies, and state and local health agencies to assure the safety of our food supply. Despite its size, the FDA has not been able to keep pace with the growth and complexity of the food production industry. Many domestic food processing plants are not visited by an inspector more than once every five years. The FDA is also charged with inspection of the imported food supply, which has grown rapidly in recent decades. Many of these

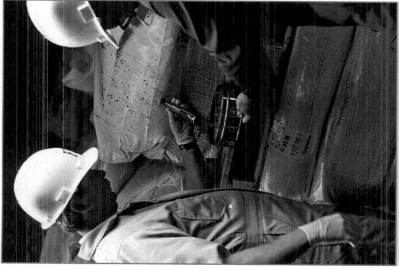

FIGURE 1.6 Consumer safety officers Dean Cook and Matthew M. Henciak, members of the FDA's Office of Regulatory Affairs' Baltimore District import operations group, inspect spices at the port of Baltimore in 2000.

imported foods come from countries with inadequate controls over production methods, yet it is impossible for the FDA to inspect all foods entering the United States. In 2006, FDA inspectors sampled less than 3% of the food shipments that arrived at American ports.

In addition to the FDA's primary goal of preventing any contamination of our food supply, the FDA is also active in responding to evidence of any failure of the safety network. It works closely with the Centers for Disease Control and Prevention (CDC) in cases of suspected disease outbreaks related to food sources. Computer networks among the 50 states are available to react quickly in the event of food-related illnesses. Efforts are underway to expand the FDA's reach in light of the increasing seriousness of growing food scares and to deal with the ever more complex food supply system.

U.S. Department of Agriculture

The U.S. Department of Agriculture (USDA) is responsible for overseeing the approximately 20% of our food supply provided by meat, poultry, and eggs. They work to assure that these products

FIGURE 1.7 Juana Plascencia and Neomi Morrales sort and remove damaged eggs after they have been pasteurized at the National Pasteurized Eggs processing facility in 2006 in Lansing, Illinois. The pasteurization process destroys viruses, including avian influenza, and harmful bacteria, including *Salmonella*.

are safe, wholesome, and correctly packaged. America is a nation of meat eaters; the average person eats more than 200 pounds (91 kilograms) of meat each year. Unfortunately, meat and poultry products are at high risk of contamination by bacteria that can cause illness. Meat processing is a tough and dirty business, just as it was in the days when Upton Sinclair exposed its practices in *The Jungle*. The USDA oversees inspection of meatpacking and poultry processing plants, and the testing for contaminants that could cause illness. In cooperation with other agencies, they respond to evidence of illnesses caused by consumption of meat products. Consumer education about nutrition and food safety is a major part of their mission. Much of the foodborne illness caused by meat, poultry, and egg products can be eliminated through careful cleaning during food preparation and thorough cooking.

Centers for Disease Control and Prevention

As the major agency responsible for monitoring health and disease, the Centers for Disease Control and Prevention (CDC) develops disease prevention strategies that are based on sound scientific evidence, monitors ongoing health problems, develops public health policies, and promotes healthy behaviors. It provides expertise to local health agencies and has emergency teams ready to go into the field in cases of major outbreaks of foodborne illness. Through its Office of Food Safety, it keeps track of individual cases of foodborne illness and partners with other agencies to investigate outbreaks. The CDC estimates that as many as 76 million people in the United States experience a foodborne illness each year, and approximately 5,000 die from it. The CDC operates the FoodNet survey system to monitor the impact of foodborne illnesses on public health. These illnesses are difficult to track accurately because many cases are never reported. Also, it may not be clear in particular cases if an illness was due to a food or water source, or if it was spread by some other means.

Environmental Protection Agency

The Environmental Protection Agency (EPA) is responsible for protecting the American public from any health risks caused by eating foods contaminated with **pesticides**. Before any new pesticide can be applied to a food crop, it must be thoroughly tested for safety and approved by the EPA. The pesticide can only be used on the specified crop and must be applied in the manner approved by the EPA. Pesticides play a major role in modern agriculture, protecting crops from the effects of weeds, insects, fungi, and rodents.

Even when pesticides are applied as approved by the EPA, small amounts of the chemicals may remain on fruits, veg-

COUNTING THE CASES

Most cases of foodborne illness are so mild that the individual does not consult a physician. No testing is done to determine what organism caused the illness, and no public health system is notified. Yet the CDC estimates that 76 million people are affected each year in the United States. How do scientists have any idea of the numbers of cases of infection, and how many are due to various types of pathogens? Since 1996, the CDC has operated FoodNet, the Foodborne Diseases Active Surveillance Network. It represents a cooperative effort among the CDC, USDA, FDA, and 10 state health departments. Its purpose is to provide accurate and ongoing estimates of the extent of foodborne diseases in the United States, to provide a breakdown of infections by type of pathogen, and to monitor trends in illness over time. The geographic areas in the survey include more than 15% of the population.

Data are collected on all laboratory-confirmed positive specimens for nine food-related pathogens, along with information on the person's age, gender, and whether the illness resulted in hospitalization. This information is supplemented by surveys of physicians, laboratories, and the general population within the study areas. Using these additional data, researchers are able to estimate, for each positive specimen, how many other people see their physicians without undergoing specimen testing, and how many people in the general population are sick with a suspected foodborne illness but do not visit their physician. Statistical methods incorporating these data allow researchers to estimate the extent and types of foodborne illnesses in the entire U.S. population. The information allows the CDC to take actions aimed at disease prevention where they will have the largest impact. Also, the information allows them to track the impact of their interventions based on whether numbers of cases of illness go up or down following the intervention. In recent years, the numbers have remained fairly constant, suggesting that further interventions are needed in order to reduce the impact of foodborne illnesses.

etables, or grains. As a result, traces of pesticides may be on the fresh produce that reaches the consumer, or in processed foods sold at the grocery store. The EPA sets maximum allowable levels of pesticides that may remain on or in foods. These levels are set many times lower than what tests indicate could actually harm human health. The FDA and USDA are responsible for monitoring pesticides in foods to be sure the allowable levels are not exceeded.

The EPA is responsible for setting safety standards for public water supplies. They determine what levels of chemicals may safely be present in drinking water without causing risk to human health. An EPA hotline provides information to consumers about drinking water quality.

CONSUMER'S ROLE IN FOOD SAFETY

Starting in the thirteenth century, English bakers worked under laws that controlled the quality and price of bread. There followed a succession of laws that regulated food suppliers and brewers of early England. English colonists in America brought with them the expectation that their food sources would be regulated to assure quality. But food safety laws in colonial America were spotty at best, as all decisions about regulating food safety were left up to local governments. It was not until the Pure Food and Drug Act of 1906 that a serious attempt was made to control food safety at the federal level. Since that time, food safety regulation has been a cat-and-mouse game between a fast-growing food industry and government regulators. Although the vast majority of food producers are honest and concerned for the public health, making a profit is the chief aim of all of them. This has often led producers to cut corners by overlooking unsanitary processing methods or using lesser-quality foods. And even under strict government guidelines, it is impossible for inspectors to be everywhere in every food production plant to be sure the rules are followed.

To protect themselves, today's food consumers need to learn more about food safety topics. Educated consumers can support funding for research about food hazards. They can demand better government regulation and increased funding for additional food inspectors. Food choices can be made for a diet that provides good nutrition and also considers food safety. It might mean opting for more expensive cuts of meat or choosing fresh produce instead of highly processed sources. Other steps for safer food include using a cooler bag to keep foods chilled on trips home from the grocery store, washing produce well, storing food properly according to recommendations for the particular food type, always cooking meats to recommended temperatures, and cleaning kitchen surfaces thoroughly.

Restaurants pose their own special problems for the consumer who is concerned with food safety. Restaurants are inspected by local health departments, and it is possible to check these records for violations. Any evidence of unsanitary conditions should provide enough reason to choose another restaurant. Hot foods served buffet-style should be hot, not lukewarm. If any food tastes or smells spoiled, it should not be eaten.

REVIEW

Foodborne illnesses continue to pose a serious threat to public health, despite centuries of efforts to combat them. Conversion from a farm-based economy in which most people grew their own food to our modern food production and delivery system has created new threats to the food supply. Among these are pesticide residues, antibiotic use in meat production, food additives in manufactured foods, and newly emerging **microorganisms.** Media coverage at the beginning of the twentieth century focused public attention on the safety of their food supply. The resulting outcry prompted the first major federal regulation of the food industry. Several government agencies now share responsibilities to protect the public from foodborne and waterborne illnesses. Consumers also play an essential role in protecting themselves from possible contaminants in their foods.

2

CAUSES OF FOODBORNE ILLNESSES

Any illness that results from consuming contaminated foods or beverages is classified as a foodborne illness. Most cases are mild, consisting of little more than a few days of nausea, vomiting, and perhaps diarrhea. Still, considering that millions of people experience mild bouts of foodborne illness each year, there is a high human cost in terms of lost school or work time. Scientists recognize more than 250 kinds of foodborne illness, and some of them cause much more serious damage to health. New sources of illness continue to be discovered as microorganisms spread around the world through increasing trade, new microorganisms evolve, food production and consumption habits change, and improved testing identifies previously unrecognized sources.

Most kinds of foodborne illness cause **gastroenteritis**, which is an inflammation of the stomach and intestinal linings and is to blame for the unpleasant symptoms of foodborne illness. Young children, pregnant women, the elderly, and those with weakened immune systems or certain other medical disorders are more likely to contract serious illness from eating contaminated food.

Digestive System

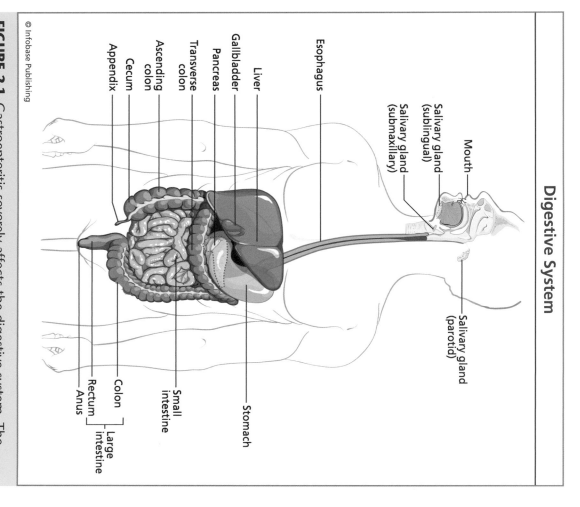

Mouth

Salivary gland (sublingual)

Salivary gland (submaxillary)

Salivary gland (parotid)

Esophagus

Liver

Gallbladder

Pancreas

Transverse colon

Ascending colon

Cecum

Appendix

Stomach

Small intestine

Colon

Rectum

Anus

Large intestine

FIGURE 2.1 Gastroenteritis severely affects the digestive system. The inflammation of the gastrointestinal tract, involving both the stomach and small intestine, results in severe diarrhea. The inflammation is typically caused by an infection by certain viruses or omit less frequently bacteria.

Most foodborne illnesses are caused by tiny living organisms that are classified as bacteria, viruses, or parasites. The human environment is full of such organisms, and most of them are harmless. Some are even helpful, in fact essential, in enabling our bodies to function. But a few of these organisms can make us sick if we accidentally eat food that is contaminated with them. Organisms that can cause infection are sometimes referred to as **pathogens**. After eating food contaminated with pathogens, or "bad bugs," it takes a while for a person to begin to feel sick. This delay is called the incubation period. This period may last only a few hours or as much as several days; it depends on the particular bug and how much contaminated food was eaten. The bugs begin to multiply while still in the stomach. Once they make their way into the intestines, they attach to the intestinal walls where they continue to multiply. They are shed in the feces. This is why hand washing is important after using the toilet. A person's feces may contain infectious pathogens for many days after he or she has otherwise recovered from an illness.

Most organisms do their damage by taking up temporary residence in the cells lining the intestinal walls. Others attack the body by producing a **toxin** (poison) that is absorbed into the bloodstream. A few types of organisms are able to penetrate the intestinal walls and invade other parts of the body. These cause the most serious cases of foodborne illness. Fortunately, they are rare. It is not possible to know for sure what organism is the cause of a particular illness unless a physician takes a specimen and orders laboratory tests.

On occasion, poisonous substances, or toxins, find their way into our food sources. Depending on the substance and the amount of it that is eaten, mild or very serious illness can result. In some cases, these toxins are the products of bacteria that are able to live in certain foods and produce the toxins. Other chemicals that act as poisons in the human body may enter foods on the farm or in processing plants. For example, fruits and vegetables may be contaminated with pesticides used to protect the crop from pests. Certain mushrooms naturally contain substances that are toxic to humans. In fact, the common name of toadstool for an inedible mushroom comes from a German word meaning

EATING FOR THE THRILL OF IT

Most people eat because they are hungry, or because they like the taste of a particular food. Yet some people enjoy flirting with danger by feasting on a Japanese meal of puffer fish. These strange-looking fish are able to puff themselves up into an inedible-looking balloon shape to avoid being eaten by predators. As an added defense, their bodies also harbor a poison in the liver, skin, and gonads that is a thousand times more toxic than cyanide. This poison is a neurotoxin, which means it affects the nervous system of anyone who eats it. The first symptoms may include a tingling in the mouth or lips, followed by dizziness and tingling in the arms and legs. Depending on how much of the poison is eaten, paralysis and even death may result.

In Japan, people can pay hundreds of dollars for the privilege of dining on this delicacy. It is available only in special restaurants where highly trained chefs have been certified in how to prepare the fish, carefully removing the organs that contain the poison. Some say that chefs may leave a tiny bit of the toxin in the fish so that diners will get the thrill of having a numb mouth and lips and enjoy their close brush with death! Despite rigorous government regulations, a few people still die each year from a meal of this traditional Japanese delicacy. In the United States, the FDA has issued an advisory regarding puffer fish that severely restricts their sale.

FIGURE 2.2 The unique-looking puffer fish's means of defense—the ability to harbor poison in its body—makes it a daring meal for humans.

"death's stool." Wild mushrooms should not be eaten unless they have been identified as safe by a trained expert.

SOURCES OF SOME COMMON FOODBORNE ILLNESSES

Campylobacter

Campylobacter is the leading source of bacterial foodborne diarrhea in the United States. The bacteria are often present in the intestinal tracts of healthy chickens and turkeys. They are a common contaminant of raw poultry sold in grocery stores. *Campylobacter* may also occur in raw milk and untreated drinking water. Infection by these bacteria is one of the most preventable foodborne illnesses. The bacteria can be destroyed by cooking foods to the proper temperatures. This is why it is so important to be sure that chicken and turkey are well cooked, either in home cooking or when eating in restaurants. It is essential to wash hands and kitchen surfaces thoroughly after preparing raw chicken or turkey.

Bacteria may be transferred between individuals due to inadequate hygiene. Although several million people become sick from *Campylobacter* each year, the majority of cases are mild. Cases are more common in the summer months. The use of antibiotics to promote growth of poultry can lead to strains of *Campylobacter* that are resistant to powerful antibiotics. Persons who get sick from consuming these resistant forms are more likely to get very sick and end up in the hospital. In rare cases, *Campylobacter* infection may cause a person to develop Guillain-Barré syndrome, a disorder in which the body's immune system attacks the nerve cells; it sometimes leads to paralysis.

Salmonella

Bacteria in the *Salmonella* family are responsible for several types of foodborne illness and have been the cause of the typhoid fever outbreaks that have plagued civilization throughout history. They were implicated in the infamous "Typhoid Mary" incident in which a woman was hospitalized against her will for years because the public was so in fear of the disease she spread. Modern sanitary water and sewer systems have largely controlled the spread of typhoid fever.

Another type of *Salmonella* infection continues to be a major public health problem. The disease caused by these bacteria is usually less serious than typhoid. However, the bacteria have proved very hard to control and are widespread among all forms of livestock, especially poultry and pigs. Disease can spread to humans if contamination from animal feces comes in contact with a food source. *Salmonella* bacteria are responsible for many large outbreaks of foodborne illness. A huge variety of foods can be affected. Outbreaks have led to major food recalls after investigators were

FIGURE 2.3 Lou Tousignant (*left*) of Minneapolis, Minnesota, who lost his father to food poisoning, and Peter Hurley of Wilsonville, Oregon, testify during a hearing before the U.S. Congress on February 11, 2009. The House Energy and Commerce Committee sought information about recent *Salmonella* outbreaks associated with peanut butter manufactured by the Peanut Corporation of America.

able to trace the illness to its source. *Salmonella* contamination has also occurred in a municipal water supply. Each year, a few hundred people in the United States die from *Salmonella* infection.

In 1994, a *Salmonella* outbreak that was eventually traced to contaminated ice cream sickened 220,000. In 2009, the FDA ordered the recall of a huge number of products that contained peanut butter from a particular processing plant. There was a chance that any processed foods made from products from that plant had become contaminated with *Salmonella*.

Eggs are one of the most common sources of intestinal illness due to *Salmonella*. Chickens infected with the bacteria lay eggs that contain the organisms within the eggshell. New government regulations aim to reduce the hazard to consumers, but it is nevertheless wise to keep eggs refrigerated before use and to cook them thoroughly.

A new form of *Salmonella* infection is of particular concern to health care workers. This is because the organisms have developed resistance to powerful antibiotics used to treat *Salmonella* food poisoning. Farmers and ranchers routinely administer antibiotics to healthy livestock in order to keep them healthy and to promote growth. While these antibiotics kill most of the bacteria living in an animal's digestive tract, a few of the bacteria will prove to be resistant. These antibiotic-resistant bacteria can then multiply and may eventually contaminate a human food source. The antibiotics that are used to treat human illness will be ineffective against the new antibiotic-resistant organisms. Many scientists and consumer groups recommend a prohibition against antibiotic use in healthy livestock in order to reduce the chances of foodborne antibiotic-resistant "superbugs" making their way into our food system.

Escherichia coli (E. coli)

The majority of the many varieties of *E. coli* bacteria are completely harmless. Only a few varieties are of concern because of their ability to cause human illness. One variety of *E. coli* occurs rarely in the United States but is well known to travelers

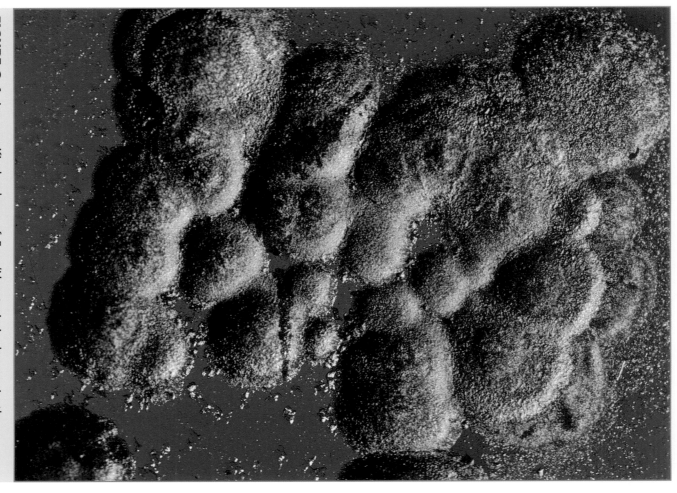

FIGURE 2.4 A magnified colony of *E. coli* bacteria is shown. In the human body, some varieties of the bacteria can cause temporary intestinal problems, kidney failure, and even death as organs shut down.

in less-developed countries. "Travelers' diarrhea" is most often caused by a form called enterotoxigenic *E. coli*. Travelers to countries where this disease occurs are warned to avoid tap water, raw fruits and vegetables, and undercooked meat and seafood. This form of *E. coli* illness is rarely life threatening and is usually over in one or two days.

One form of *E. coli*, O157:H7, is a major health concern in the United States. The genetic structure of bacteria allows them to easily take on new characteristics. At some point, a new variety of *E. coli* developed that had the characteristic of causing severe illness in humans. This type of *F. coli* lives harmlessly in the intestines of cows. However, it has a quite different effect in the intestines of humans where it invades the gastrointestinal walls and produces damaging toxins. These toxins are capable of causing bleeding from the intestinal walls, resulting in bloody diarrhea, a characteristic symptom of the disease. A very small number of these bacteria, perhaps as few as 10, can cause a person to become sick.

Once scientists identified this variety of *E. coli*, they gave it the name *E. coli* O157:H7. This organism came to public attention in 1993 when hundreds of customers of the popular Jack in the Box hamburger chain got sick after eating meat contaminated with it. Since then, it has been responsible for disease outbreaks associated with lettuce, spinach, and other foods. It was also the contaminant in the hamburger that left Stephanie Smith paralyzed (see Chapter 1). Most of the news reports about *E. coli* outbreaks are referring to the O157:H7 form.

Vibrio

One type of *Vibrio* bacteria (*Vibrio vulnificus*) commonly occurs in the warm coastal waters of the United States. Oysters, clams, and crabs harvested from these waters may be contaminated with *Vibrio*. Contamination is more common in the summer months because of warmer water temperatures. Well-cooked shellfish from these waters are safe to eat since the bacteria are killed by heat. But those who like to eat raw oysters face a risk of coming down with a *Vibrio* infection. *Vibrio* bacteria in the gastrointestinal tract can invade the bloodstream, leading to serious illness and even death. Each year in the United States, several people die after eating raw oysters. Persons with liver disease or compromised immune systems are at greatest risk from *Vibrio* infection. The FDA cautions such persons against eating raw or undercooked shellfish.

Another variety of *Vibrio* (*Vibrio cholerae*) is the cause of cholera. Cholera epidemics have been feared for centuries because of how rapidly the disease can spread through a population. Within hours of infection, patients may become seriously ill and even die, due to rapid dehydration. The *Vibrio* bacteria produce a toxin that causes the severe watery diarrhea that is characteristic of cholera. The disease is spread by fecal contamination of the food and water supply. It remains a threat in parts of the world with inadequate sanitation. Cholera rarely occurs in the United States, and many of the reported cases involve individuals who have just returned from foreign travel.

Listeria

Listeria infection is a serious disease because the bacteria are able to penetrate the intestinal lining. Once in the bloodstream, the bacteria can multiply and infect other organs. Pregnant women are at particular risk for *Listeria* infection. The bacteria are able to cross the placental barrier and infect the fetus, resulting in miscarriage. *Listeria* contamination is most likely to occur in raw meats and unpasteurized dairy products. The bacteria are killed by cooking, but occasionally, processed foods, such as cold cuts, become contaminated again after cooking. Soft cheeses made from unpasteurized milk are of particular concern for *Listeria* contamination. Efforts in the food processing industry have resulted in a reduction in *Listeria* infections. Still, an estimated 2,500 people are infected by *Listeria* in the United States annually, and about 500 deaths result.

Norovirus

Norovirus may also be called Norwalk virus or Norwalk-like virus. This family of viruses is one of the most common causes of foodborne illness. The disease it causes is often referred to as the "stomach flu" (but it is not related to influenza). The virus is very contagious and can spread quickly through child care centers or nursing homes. Viruses differ from bacteria in that they are not able to multiply in a contaminated food source. Spread of the virus is usually by transfer from an infected person. This may occur due to improper hand washing by food handlers after using the toilet. An individual may also pick up the virus by touching a contaminated surface and then putting the hand in the mouth. Shellfish may become contaminated if they are near a sewage discharge. The threat of illness from shellfish may be eliminated by proper cooking. A case of norovirus infection is usually over after one or two days, but the feces may spread the disease for at least another three days after recovery.

Rotavirus

Infection with rotavirus is the major cause of severe diarrhea among very young children. It can be spread by an infected food handler who fails to follow proper hand-washing methods. It may also be spread among infants in child-care settings through improper diaper handling. Since the introduction in 2006 of infant vaccination against rotavirus, the number of cases has dropped in the United States. However, rotavirus remains a significant cause of illness and death among infants in less-developed countries.

Shigella

Young children are at highest risk of infection from *Shigella* bacteria. The disease is most often spread from person to person. Thorough hand washing by those infected, by food handlers, and by child-care workers can prevent the spread of infection. Contamination may occur in raw produce that is grown in fields near sewage. Water sources and children's play pools can be contaminated with *Shigella*. Most people soon recover completely from *Shigella* infection. However, a few sufferers develop arthritis, a painful disease of the joints.

Entamoeba histolytica

Amoeba are tiny, one-celled parasitic organisms. *Entamoeba histolytica* is a type of amoeba that is able to infect humans and is spread through fecal contamination of food or water. It is a major cause of dysentery, or severe diarrhea. While uncommon in the United States, it is a major health problem in less-developed tropical countries where sanitation is poor.

Giardia

Giardia are tiny, single-celled parasites that are most frequently spread through contaminated water. Their tough outer shell allows them to survive for months in the environment. Campers and backpackers are warned not to drink the water from streams or lakes because it may be contaminated with *Giardia*. Occasionally, municipal water supplies become contaminated with *Giardia*. The nausea and diarrhea associated with infection usually go away within two weeks. Some people who contract *Giardia* infection experience no symptoms and do not know they are infected. Nevertheless, they can act as carriers of disease through the possibility of fecal contamination.

Hepatitis A Virus

Hepatitis A is a liver disease caused by a foodborne virus. Food contamination generally occurs through food handlers who are careless about sanitation practices. Beverages, seafood, and salads are frequent sources of outbreaks. The incubation period before the first symptoms appear is quite long, up to 50 days. During this time, an infected individual may be a contagious source of the virus and not know it. The illness is generally mild, characterized by fever, nausea, and abdominal discomfort. Children who are infected may not show any symptoms. It is estimated that a few thousand people get hepatitis A each year in the United States, but the number is decreasing. A vaccine to prevent hepatitis A infection became available in 1995. Vaccination is recommended for all infants.

Clostridium

Clostridium botulinum bacteria produce a strong toxin capable of causing severe food poisoning. The toxin may occur in home-canned foods that are not properly processed and that are not reheated before eating. Only a few dozen cases occur each year in the United States, but some of these result in death.

Another variety of *Clostridium* (*C. perfringens*) is the cause of a much more common form of foodborne illness. Abdominal cramping and diarrhea result from a toxin produced by the bacteria. Symptoms are usually over within one day. Precooked meat products stored at improper temperatures are usually the source of *C. perfringens* contamination. Places such as schools and hospitals that prepare large quantities of food in advance are the most common sources of this infection.

Mad Cow Disease

This disease was first reported in British cows in the 1980s. It got its name from the odd behavior of cows that were sickened with the disease. Its scientific name, bovine spongiform encephalopathy (BSE), comes from the spongy appearance of the brain of infected animals. During the 1990s, doctors noted an increase in an extremely rare human disease called Creutzfeldt-Jakob disease (CJD), in particular among young people. This disease leads to deterioration of the nervous system, loss of muscle control, and, eventually, death. The cause remained a mystery for some time, but doctors noticed a connection between mad cow disease and CJD in humans. Finally, they identified the cause as a new form of infectious agent called a prion. This agent is capable of infecting livestock and humans. Prions are able to change the body's normal proteins to abnormal shapes, resulting in disease. It is believed that prions were spread among livestock through the practice of feeding animals with discarded products from butchering. Since this practice was stopped, the disease has rarely recurred, although monitoring continues and outbreaks have been reported. The first U.S. case was reported in 2003.

SOME NOTABLE OUTBREAKS OF FOODBORNE ILLNESSES

City and county health departments are on the front line when it comes to detecting new outbreaks of foodborne illnesses. Our centralized food production system often leads to simultaneous outbreaks in several states. As soon as the widespread nature of an outbreak is recognized, the federal CDC steps in to coordinate investigations. A network of health agencies immediately begins the difficult process of collecting information on illnesses. Persons with food-poisoning symptoms are asked to fill out a lengthy questionnaire about foods they have eaten in the previous week. These questionnaires are compared to look

FIGURE 2.5 An Iraqi girl fills a tin with drinking water from a water pipe crossing an uncovered sewage canal in Fdailiyah, Iraq, in December 2007. At that time, many Iraqi neighborhoods lacked essential infrastructure, such as electricity and clean water, due to war-time conditions. The United Nations warned of a cholera outbreak after at least 101 cases were reported in the capital city of Baghdad in just three weeks.

for foods that all the subjects have eaten. Once suspicion falls on a particular food source, investigators try to obtain as many samples of it as possible. (Investigations are often held up at this point, since it may be impossible to obtain samples of foods that were eaten many days before.) Any available food samples are submitted to laboratories that can determine the **DNA fingerprint** of suspected disease-causing organisms. When these genetic fingerprints have pinpointed a particular food source as the culprit, the FDA and USDA use their regulatory powers to alert the media and to recommend recalls of the affected foods. Once the outbreak has been controlled, the CDC continues to collect information that may help to prevent future outbreaks.

Salmonella in Peanut Butter

In the fall of 2008, sporadic reports of *Salmonella* food poisoning began to arrive at health departments in several states. As cases accumulated, the CDC was called in to begin the investigative process to identify a common food source. By January 2009, attention centered on peanut butter as a possible source of *Salmonella* contamination. However, before a product recall could take place, the original place of contamination had to be identified. Finally, the trail led the FDA inspectors to a Peanut Corporation of America plant, which turned out to be the source of the *Salmonella* contamination. A warning was sent out to consumers across the country, and a recall was issued for products made by the company. This recall was later expanded and, in the end, involved more than 1,500 products that contained peanut butter from the Peanut Corporation of America. Eventually, more than 700 people in 46 states were sickened by the contaminated peanut butter. Follow up investigations by the FDA found evidence suggesting that the Peanut Corporation of America was aware of *Salmonella* contamination at their plant in Blakely, Georgia. The original source may have been from bird feces that entered the production area through a leaky roof.

E. coli O157:H7 in Ground Beef Patties

Beginning in the summer of 2007, several people came down with food poisoning caused by *E. coli* O157:H7 bacteria. Because this variety of *E. coli* is a rare food contaminant, the cases immediately came to the attention of public health officials. DNA fingerprints of samples from ill persons were compared to the DNA of *E. coli* strains found in samples of frozen beef patties obtained from patients' homes. A match was found with patties produced by the Topps Meat Company. A recall notice

THE FIVE-SECOND RULE FLUNKS THE TEST

You've probably done it; almost everyone has. You drop a piece of candy, pick it up right away and shout (or think) "Five-second rule!" just before you pop it in your mouth. It is a nice little lie that makes us feel better even though we know the candy might very well have picked up some dirt or germs from its few seconds on the floor.

High-school student Jillian Clarke decided to test the "five-second rule": Could a piece of candy actually pick up bacteria in such a short time? She designed an experiment and worked with scientists at the University of Illinois to carry it out. In place of the floor, she used ceramic tiles she purchased at a hardware store. After smearing the tiles with (non-pathogenic) *E. coli* bacteria, she put gummy bears and cookies on the tiles, and then waited five seconds before removing them. Every sample of cookie or candy picked up bacteria from the tiles. Jillian also surveyed people about the five-second rule and found that women were more likely to eat food dropped on the floor than men. She also found that candy is much more likely than broccoli to be picked up and eaten. Jillian's research on the five-second rule won her the 2004 Ig Nobel Award from the *Annals of Improbable Research*.

was issued for 21.7 million pounds (9.8 million kg) of ground beef produced by Topps. At least 35 people in eight states fell ill. Most of them were hospitalized, and two developed kidney failure.

This was one of a series of recalls of foods that were found to be contaminated with *E. coli* O157:H7. In addition to ground beef, *E. coli* O157:H7 has been found in fresh produce and in cookie dough. Consumer groups have called for greater government surveillance that can track meat products back to the slaughter-

Dr. Paul Dawson and his students at Clemson University extended Jillian's research. They set out to answer several other questions: Does the type of surface or kind of food matter? Do foods pick up more bacteria if they are left on the surface longer? Are there enough bacteria on them to make someone sick? They used *Salmonella* bacteria on tile, wood, and carpet surfaces. The foods tested were bread and bologna. They found that food left on any surface for five seconds picked up from 150 to 8,000 bacteria. Food left longer than five seconds picked up more bacteria. Would this be enough to make someone sick? It could, depending on the type of bacteria.

Dr. Dawson and his students also decided to test whether "double dipping" while eating chips and dips leads to bacterial contamination. Double dipping is when someone dips, say, a potato chip into dip, takes a bite from the chip, then sticks it back in the bowl for more. The researchers set out various types of dips and invited people to bite into chips before placing them into the dips. When the dips were tested, results showed that thousands of bacteria had been transferred from people's mouths into the dips. In the words of Dr. Dawson, "I like to say it's like kissing everybody at the party—if you're double dipping, you're putting some of your bacteria in that dip."

FIGURE 2.6 While demonstrating in front of USDA headquarters, Nancy Donley of Safe Tables Our Priority (*right*) explains how her son died as a result of eating *E. coli*-contaminated ground beef.

houses where the contaminant originates. Health agencies have redoubled efforts to educate consumers on the importance of cooking ground beef patties until they are well done.

GROUPS AT HIGH RISK FOR FOODBORNE ILLNESS

Diabetes

It is estimated that nearly 8% of Americans have some form of diabetes, although many are not aware that they have it. Diabetes is a disease that interferes with the body's ability to produce or use insulin. A side effect of the disease is that the immune system does not work as well as it should to fight off disease. When diabetics consume foods that are contaminated with disease-causing organisms, their immune system may not be able to protect them from foodborne illnesses. Diabetics must be especially careful to follow recommended food storage and preparation procedures and to avoid undercooked poultry, meat, and eggs.

Pregnancy

During pregnancy, a woman's immune system undergoes changes. These changes occur naturally and are designed to protect both the woman and the developing fetus. Some of the changes make women more susceptible to foodborne illness. This is why women are cautioned to be very careful about the foods they eat when pregnant. Infection with *Listeria* bacteria is of particular concern to pregnant women. The bacteria can be passed to the fetus and lead to miscarriage or death of the newborn. According to the CDC, pregnant women are 20 times more likely to get sick from *Listeria* contamination than other healthy adults.

Acquired Immune Deficiency Virus (AIDS)

The AIDS virus causes disease by damaging the human immune system. (Doctors may refer to the resulting damage as a compromised immune system.) Persons with AIDS are not able to fight off invading organisms, such as those coming from contaminated food, as well as a healthy person. For this reason, they must be extra careful about the foods they eat. Recommended procedures for food handling and cooking must be strictly followed.

Liver Disease

Persons with liver disease are cautioned against eating raw oysters that may be contaminated with *Vibrio* bacteria. Heavy drinking of alcoholic beverages may damage the liver. Persons without a fully functioning liver are less able to resist *V. vilnificus* infection if they are exposed to the organism.

REVIEW

Illnesses that are spread through foods or beverages are most often the result of infection with bacteria, viruses, or parasites. Biological toxins and other poisonous chemicals may also cause illness if they are ingested in sufficient amounts. The most commonly recognized foodborne infections are associated with the bacteria *Campylobacter*, *Salmonella*, and *E. coli* O157:H7, or the family of viruses referred to as noroviruses. Most illnesses are mild cases of gastroenteritis, but each year, thousands of people experience much more serious forms of illness, resulting in hospitalization and even death. Certain populations are at higher risk of foodborne illness, including the very old, the very young, pregnant women, and those with compromised immune systems or certain chronic diseases.

3

FOOD ALLERGIES AND FOOD INTOLERANCE

Some children can enjoy a peanut butter and jelly sandwich every day. Others cannot even be in the same room with a peanut butter sandwich. The reason is that some children are highly allergic to peanuts. Still, peanuts are not the only source of food allergies. In fact, there are many other foods that, while tasty and nutritious for most people, may actually cause serious reactions in a small number of others.

One of about every 25 children in the United States experiences some kind of allergic reaction to food every year. Allergies are less common among teenagers and adults. The symptom of a food allergy can be as minor as a case of hives or a tingling sensation in the mouth. Itchy eyes, vomiting, and diarrhea can also be signs of food allergy. The types of symptoms are person-specific rather than food-specific. Two people may be allergic to fish but show much different allergy symptoms. In contrast to illness that is caused by eating contaminated food, allergy symptoms can occur within minutes after eating the allergy-causing food. Occasionally, people with severe allergies may experience **anaphylaxis**, or an anaphylactic reaction, if they inadvertently eat the food that triggers their allergy. Anaphylaxis is a life-threatening condition characterized by a drop in blood pressure, rapid swelling in the face or throat region, and difficulty breathing. Each year in the United States, 30,000 people are rushed to emergency rooms because of anaphylactic reactions to food.

THE ABCS OF FOOD ALLERGIES

Our immune system is made up of a complex set of organs, cells, and chemicals that protect our bodies from "foreign" substances. Cells of the immune system circulate throughout the body, ready to attack bacteria, viruses, or toxic chemicals that find their way inside. We usually think of our immune systems as helping us to fight off the type of organisms that cause sore throats, wound infections, or even food poisoning. Our digestive systems have developed a special form of immune system that is able to recognize most substances in the foods we eat as safe, even though they are otherwise foreign to the body. The normally functioning immune system does not mount an immune response when these foods pass through the intestinal tract. The foods are broken down by the digestive system, and essential nutrients are absorbed by the body, all without triggering a reaction by the immune system.

A food allergy is a reaction by the body's immune system against a food substance that most people can eat with no ill effect. The particular chemical substance in the food that causes the immune system to react is called an **allergen**. For example, peanuts contain several forms of proteins, in addition to fats and micronutrients. The chemical structures of some peanut proteins are recognized as allergens by some people's immune systems. As a result, these people develop an allergic reaction if they ingest peanuts.

At birth, an infant's immune system is not fully developed. Over the child's first three years, the child's immune system develops as it learns to tolerate new foods introduced into the diet. But sometimes, something goes wrong during this development process—the immune system may start reacting to a particular food substance as being foreign. When this happens, the immune cells mount a response to this foreign invader by producing specialized proteins called **antibodies**. One type of antibody that plays an important role in producing the allergic response is called IgE. These IgE antibodies cause the release of biologically active chemicals that spread throughout the body. This is part of the body's normal response to protect itself against threatening substances. But in the case of allergies, the food substance is actually harmless, and the immune response is inappropriate. The chemicals produced by the immune system cause the damage that brings on the symptoms of food allergy. The symptoms may occur in the skin, respiratory tract, or gastrointestinal tract, depending on the individual.

Until a few decades ago, many doctors did not believe that babies could suffer from food allergies. Much has been learned since then, and researchers continue to learn more about what causes food allergies and how they can be prevented. We now know that the genetic codes inherited from the parents play a role in whether a particular baby's developing immune system will show normal or allergic responses to food. Babies born to parents with allergies are more likely to develop food allergies. In addition, a mother's diet during her pregnancy and the timing of introduction of new foods into the baby's diet may play a role in training the immune system to tolerate changes in diet. Researchers continue to study the process by which infants learn to tolerate new foods in order to tell new mothers how best to prevent the occurrence of allergies in their infants. The American Academy of Pediatrics recommends that infants at high risk of allergies (for instance, those whose parents or siblings have allergies) be exclusively breast-fed for at least four months. They further recommend that parents delay the introduction of solid foods until the infant is four to six months of age.

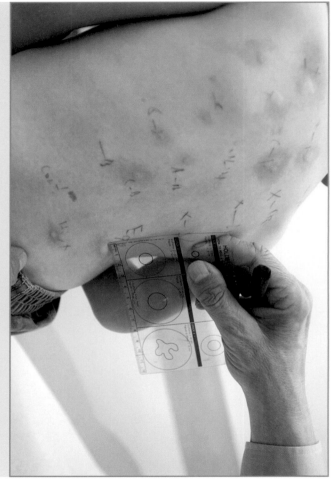

FIGURE 3.1 A doctor performs a skin-prick test on a toddler. The test is done by placing a drop of a solution containing an allergen on the skin and then making a series of scratches or pricks to enable the solution to enter the skin. If a raised, itchy, red bump develops, it may mean the person is allergic to a particular allergen.

TESTING FOR FOOD ALLERGIES

It can be hard to tell if a case of hives or an upset stomach is a sign of a food allergy because so many things can cause similar physical discomforts. Even if a particular food is suspected of causing an allergic reaction, how can we tell which one is the culprit? After all, we usually eat more than one variety of food. Also, the allergic reaction may depend on how the food was prepared or how much of it one eats before a reaction sets in. Family doctors who suspect that symptoms are due to a food allergy may recommend that patients visit an allergist.

Allergists are specially trained doctors who conduct allergy tests and recommend prevention measures. An allergist may do a skin-prick test to determine which foods cause an allergic response. In this test, a series of possible food allergens is applied just under the skin using a small pricking device. The skin area is then observed for the appearance of raised, reddened areas. These will suggest which foods are causing allergic reactions. However, the results of skin tests are not always accurate. Another test that may be required involves taking a small blood sample to test the IgE antibodies to see how they react against various foods.

Another test that can be done by the allergist is called the oral food challenge. In this test, the patient is asked to eat a sample of food that is suspected of causing an allergic reaction. This is carried out in a medical office where trained professionals are available and ready to promptly treat any allergic reaction. The elimination diet is another way to assess food allergies. Here, patients are asked to follow their usual diet for several days and keep careful records of the foods they eat and any symptoms that occur. One by one, suspected foods are eliminated from the diet. If the symptoms continue, the doctor may consider causes other than food allergies.

OUTGROWING FOOD ALLERGIES

There is a very good chance that food allergies in young children will go away after a few years. Children who are allergic to wheat, cow's milk, eggs, or soy usually outgrow it between the ages of 3 and 16 years. However, few children who are allergic to peanuts or tree nuts outgrow their allergies to these foods.

The best way to tell when someone has outgrown a food allergy is for a physician to conduct a food challenge by having the patient slowly eat a portion of the allergy-causing food. If no allergic response is observed after a few hours, this suggests that the person is no longer allergic to that particular food. Some allergy specialists recommend that persons who outgrow an allergy to peanuts eat them on a regular basis in order to maintain the body's tolerance to peanuts.

SOME COMMON CAUSES OF FOOD ALLERGY

The following eight foods are responsible for 90% of food allergies, according to the FDA. By U.S. law, packaged foods must list any of these potential allergens in the ingredient list on the package label.

Peanuts

Peanuts are not true nuts. Rather, they are in the legume family along with beans and lentils. Peanut allergy is of particular concern because of its potential to cause anaphylaxis. Some individuals are so sensitive that even breathing peanut dust or touching peanuts can result in a severe reaction. Most peanut allergies first occur in infants between one and two years of age. Only about one in

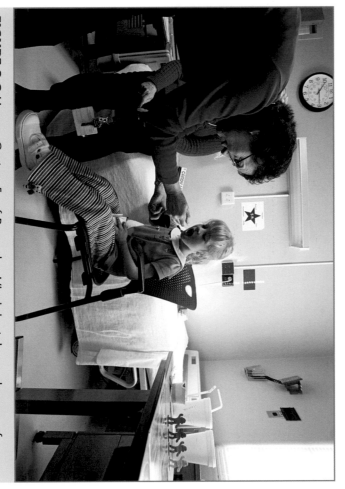

FIGURE 3.2 Hanna Carter, 5, of Roanoke, Virginia, takes a dosage of peanut protein from Nurse Practitioner Pam Steele at a clinic at Duke University in Durham, North Carolina, in March 2009. The child is being treated for peanut allergies as staff at the clinic work to retrain her immune system so she is allergy free.

LIFE IN THE PEANUT-FREE ZONE

Most children can't imagine life without peanut butter and jelly sandwiches. Yet for those with severe peanut allergies, lunch in the school cafeteria can be threatening. Severely allergic individuals find that even small exposure to peanuts could bring on anaphylactic shock and a trip to the emergency room.

Many students with peanut allergies eat lunch at special peanut-free tables in their school cafeterias or in a separate room. Their friends can eat lunch with them as long as teachers make certain there are no peanut products in their lunch boxes. Children with peanut allergies understand that they cannot accept gifts of cookies or candy, and trick-or-treating at Halloween is definitely out. They also learn that peanuts can show up in surprising places, such as when they are dropped on the ground at an outdoor event or even in gardens where peanut shells have been used in potting soils. Most likely, kids who suffer from peanut allergies will always carry an epinephrine pen (or "epi-pen") with them and know how to use it at the first sign of an anaphylactic reaction. A few children with severe allergies even have peanut-sniffing service dogs. These dogs have been trained to pick up the tiniest scent of peanut and to alert the owner to danger.

five children with a peanut allergy eventually outgrows it. Children with milder allergies are more likely to outgrow it than those with severe allergies. Persons who experience a severe reaction to peanuts may be advised to always carry an epinephrine pen. (Epinephrine is a drug used to prevent or reverse the symptoms of an anaphylactic reaction.)

Scientists have identified several proteins in peanuts that act as allergens in peanut-sensitive individuals. In addition, whether they are roasted or boiled affects how likely peanuts are to cause allergies; roasted peanuts cause more allergic reactions than unroasted peanuts. Different varieties of peanuts may be more or less allergenic. Peanut allergy is becoming more common. Researchers are studying if this may be due to how peanuts are roasted, changes in infant feeding patterns, or other causes.

Tree Nuts

There are many kinds of tree nuts, including pecan, cashew, Brazil nut, almond, and coconut. Allergy to tree nuts is fairly common, and, as with peanut allergy, there is a potential for life-threatening symptoms. Nuts are actually the seed forms of a tree, and they contain several proteins that provide the seed the ability to grow. It is these very proteins that act as allergens for people who are allergic to tree nuts. Tree nut allergies generally develop in childhood. For most people, they are a lifelong problem. Although individual persons may be strictly allergic to only one variety of tree nut, it is advised that they avoid all tree nuts and also peanuts. This is because of the potential confusion about nut varieties and also the possibility that nuts may become **cross-contaminated** in processing plants. By law, tree nuts must be identified on packaged food labels. Persons with tree nut allergies may be advised to carry an epinephrine autoinjector, often called a pen, in case they accidentally ingest a nut. Each pen contains a single injectable dose of epinephrine and must be obtained through a physician prescription.

Eggs

Egg allergy is a common allergy of childhood. Fortunately, most children outgrow it. Eggs contain many varieties of protein that act as allergens; the egg white and the yolk each contain different allergens. More children are allergic to the proteins found in egg whites. Proteins change form when they are cooked, and some children with egg allergies are able to eat well-cooked egg products. Small amounts of egg are found in many prepared foods, so the labels must be read carefully by persons who are highly allergic to eggs. However, many children can tolerate the small amounts of egg found in foods such as baked goods. Many childhood vaccines are

FIGURE 3.3 Allison Bloomfield and her son, Jack, 3, pose with an epi-pen. Bloomfield carries the pen with her at all times because her son has a peanut allergy and ingesting even just traces of peanuts can be potentially deadly.

grown in chick embryos and may contain egg protein, so a person's health care team should be informed if a patient has an egg allergy.

Milk

Many infants have an allergic reaction to proteins found in cow milk. The majority of cow milk allergies appear before the age of six months and disappear by age two. Some allergic infants are able to tolerate milk if it is boiled, but this is not always the case. Symptoms of milk allergy usually affect the skin or digestive system. It may be difficult to diagnose cow milk allergy in an infant, particularly if the symptoms appear only in the digestive tract. In this case, the problem may be lactose intolerance rather than milk allergy. Breast-fed infants may develop allergy symptoms to cow milk allergens that pass through the breast milk. In such cases, mothers are sometimes cautioned to avoid cow milk while breast-feeding their infants.

Soybeans

Soybeans are another member of the legume family. Many infants are fed soy-based formula, and a few of them develop an allergy to the formula's soy proteins. Most infants become tolerant of soy products by the age of three. The symptoms of soy protein allergy are similar to those of cow milk allergy. Often, an infant who is allergic to one of the two is also allergic to the other. Many processed foods contain soy protein. Although manufacturers are required to list soy ingredients on the package label, consumers may be confused if it is called by some other name, such as texturized vegetable protein or tofu. New labeling laws require foods containing soy products to clearly identify the soy content. Some soy-based oils may also contain soy protein and should be avoided.

Fish

Allergy to finned fish is not common, but it can result in a severe allergic reaction, and it is generally lifelong. Most people who are allergic to fish proteins react to only a single or a few varieties of fish. However, especially if there is the possibility of an anaphylac-

FIGURE 3.4 Some infants are allergic to edamame (baby soybeans in the pod) and products made from soybeans, including milk, hot dogs, and ice cream.

tic reaction, people allergic to one type of fish may want to avoid all fish. In addition, there is the possibility of cross-contamination in restaurants where the same pans or work surfaces are used for fish and other foods. The presence of fish in a prepared food is usually obvious, making it easier to avoid.

Shellfish

Allergy to shellfish usually develops in the young adult years and is generally a lifelong allergy. The two types of shellfish that cause allergies are crustaceans and mollusks. The crustacean family, which includes crabs, shrimp, and lobster, can cause severe allergic reactions. The mollusk family includes oysters, clams, mussels, and scallops. It is possible for an individual to be allergic to only one type of shellfish, but more commonly, the allergy includes several types. Medical professionals usually advise that someone who is allergic to any one type of shellfish avoid all of them. Allergens in finfish are different from those in shellfish, so persons allergic to shellfish can enjoy meals of finfish. However, restaurant meals can be risky because small amounts of shellfish may wind up in a prepared dish. There is also the likelihood of a food becoming cross-contaminated with allergenic foods on kitchen surfaces.

Sometimes, people with shellfish allergies blame the iodine in shellfish for their allergic reactions. If they require radiology testing, they worry that they will react to the iodine in the contrast agents. However, studies have shown that shellfish allergies are due to proteins in the shellfish, and not to the iodine content. Anyone with a shellfish allergy has essentially the same risk of an allergic reaction to contrast agents as someone with any other kind of allergy.

Wheat

Allergic reactions to one of the proteins found in wheat are fairly common in young children. Most children outgrow wheat allergies by age three. Children with wheat allergies are often allergic to other foods, particularly cow milk. Wheat allergies rarely occur in adults. Most individuals with wheat allergies are able to eat other grains, such as oats, corn, and rice. Sometimes, symptoms of wheat allergy occur only if a person exercises within a few hours of eating wheat. Chemical changes in the body induced by exercise can trigger or worsen an immune reaction to wheat protein. This condition may lead to life-threatening anaphylaxis.

Wheat allergy should not be confused with celiac disease, which is a serious disease in which the body reacts to the gluten portion of wheat, barley, or rye grains. Celiac disease, an autoimmune disease, is a lifelong condition in which the immune system mistakenly attacks the body's normal tissues. It is not treatable, and individuals must be very careful to avoid all forms of gluten. Otherwise, an immune reaction occurs in the presence of gluten

(continues on page 64)

THE TROUBLE WITH FOOD LABELS

If you have trouble reading food labels, you are not alone. Anyone who has puzzled over the fine print on a food package label knows how hard it is to find the information you want. Since 2006, processed food sold in the United States must say on the packaging if the food contains one of the eight major food allergens: milk, tree nuts, peanuts, soy, wheat, egg, shellfish, or fish. Common or usual food names must be used. If a food contains milk, the law requires it to say "milk" and not "casein," "whey," or other unfamiliar names that hide the presence of milk products. If a product contains tree nuts, shellfish, or fish, the label must specify the type of nut or fish. Allergens must either be included in the main list of ingredients or near the ingredient list on the label. For example, the ingredient list may be followed by the statement: "Contains soy."

Clearly, there is not a lot of room on some food package labels for all of the information that needs to be there. The FDA works with the food industry to assure that labels contain accurate nutrition and allergen information. The consumer group Center for Science in the Public Interest has stated that food manufacturers intentionally present ingredient and nutrition information in a way that is hard for consumers to decipher. The group has proposed that food manufacturers present this information in a way that is much more readable and informative. Text that uses both capital and lowercase letters would be much easier to read. Key information such as the allergen list would be highlighted in red. Red would also be used to highlight those ingredients, such as fat and sugar, which are present in excess of 20% of the recommended daily amount.

(following pages) **FIGURE 3.5** Because the current Nutrition Facts labels (*left*) are hard for some people to understand, the consumer group Center for Science in the Public Interest has recommended that the FDA change the label to a format that is easier to read and more informative (*right*).

Current Label

Nutrition Facts

Serving Size ¹⁄₁₄ Cake (107g)

Servings per Container 14

	Amount/serving	% Daily Value*
Calories 350	Calories from Fat 180	
Total Fat 14g		22%
Saturated Fat 5g		25%
Trans Fat 0g		
Cholesterol 30mg		10%
Sodium 290mg		12%
Total Carbohydrate 53g		18%
Dietary Fiber 5g		20%
Sugars 36g		
Protein 4g		

Vitamin A 0%	●	Vitamin C 0%
Calcium 4%	●	Iron 15%

*Percent Daily Values are based on a 2,000 calorie diet. Your daily values may be higher or lower depending on your calorie needs:

		Calories:	2,000	2,500
Total Fat	Less than		65g	80g
Sat Fat	Less than		20g	25g
Cholesterol	Less than		300mg	300mg
Sodium	Less than		2,400mg	2,400mg
Total Carbohydrate			300g	375g
Dietary Fiber			25g	30g

Calories per gram:
Fat 9 ● Carbohydrate 4 ● Protein 4

INGREDIENTS: ENRICHED BLEACHED FLOUR (WHEAT FLOUR, NIACIN, IRON, THIAMIN MONONITRATE, RIBOFLAVIN, FOLIC ACID), SUGAR, SKIM MILK, VEGETABLE OIL (PALM, SOYBEAN AND/OR COTTONSEED OILS), WATER, COCOA PROCESSED WITH ALKALI, EGGS, CORN SYRUP, HIGH FRUCTOSE CORN SYRUP, CHERRIES, WHITE GRAPE JUICE CONCENTRATE. CONTAINS 2% OR LESS OF EACH OF THE FOLLOWING: WHOLE WHEAT FLOUR, CARAMEL COLOR, POLYDEXTROSE, LEAVENING (BAKING SODA, SODIUM ALUMINUM PHOSPHATE, MONOCALCIUM PHOSPHATE), SALT, CORN STARCH, MONO- AND DIGLYCERIDES, NATURAL AND ARTIFICIAL FLAVORS, POLYGLYCEROL ESTERS OF FATTY ACIDS, SODIUM ALGINATE, NATURAL COCOA EXTRACT, PROPYLENE GLYCOL MONO- AND DIESTERS OF FATS AND FATTY ACIDS, MALTODEXTRIN, GELLAN GUM, LACTYLIC ESTERS OF FATTY ACIDS, SOY LECITHIN, POLYSORBATE 60, SOY FLOUR, COFFEE. **CONTAINS MILK, WHEAT, EGGS AND SOY.**

Calories and serving size should be in larger type.

Unnecessary information.

Calling it "% Daily Amount" would be more understandable.

The Daily Amount for sodium should be 1,500 mg. The current 2,400 mg is too high.

With no Daily Value for trans fat, added sugars, or protein, consumers don't know how much to shoot for each day.

"Dietary fiber" should be called "Fiber" and should include only intact fiber from whole grains, beans, vegetables, fruit, and other foods. Polydextros, maltodextrin, and similar carbohydrates should not count as fiber.

This information isn't useful for most consumers.

The label should list only added sugars (from high-fructose corn syrup, table sugar, etc.), not the naturally occurring sugars in milk and fruit.

Many people don't realize that this is ordinary refined white flour.

All-capital letters are hard to read.

Better Label

Grains: 2% whole — If the food contains grains, the label should say what percent of the grains are *whole* grains.

Nutrition Facts

Serving Size ¹/₁₄ Cake (107 g)

14 Servings per Box

Calories in 1 serving 350

Amount per serving		% Daily Amount*
Total Fat	14 g	High 22%
Saturated Fat	5 g	High 25%
Trans Fat	0 g	0%
Cholesterol	**30 mg**	**10%**
Sodium	**290 mg**	**19%**
Total Carbohydrate 53 g		**18%**
Fiber	3 g	12%
Added Sugars	30 g	High 120%
Protein	**4 g**	**8%**
Vitamin A	0%	• Vitamin C 0%
Calcium	4%	• Iron 15%

* % Daily Amount is based on 2,000 calories a day. 20% or more of the DA is HIGH. 5% or **less is LOW.**

50 mg caffeine per serving

The "% Daily Amount" lets consumers know how much of a day's worth of trans fat, added sugar, protein, etc., each serving contains.

Red color and "High" warn consumers when a serving has at least 20 percent of the Daily Amount for saturated fat, trans fat, cholesterol, sodium, or added sugars.

Caffeine content is disclosed.

Ingredient Facts

Major Ingredients: Sugars (sugar, corn syrup, high-fructose corn syrup, white grape juice concentrate) (28%) • Skim milk • Refined bleached flour (wheat flour, niacin, iron, thiamin mononitrate, riboflavin, folic acid) • Vegetable oil (palm, soybean, and/or cottonseed oils) • Water • Cocoa processed with alkali (5%) • Eggs • Cherries (3%)

Contains 2% or less of: Whole wheat flour • Caramel color • Polydextrose • Leavening (baking soda, sodium aluminum phosphate, monocalcium phosphate) • Salt • Corn starch • Mono- and diglycerides • Natural and artificial flavors • Polyglycerol esters of fatty acids • Sodium alginate • Natural cocoa extract • Propylene glycol • Mono- and diesters of fats and fatty acids • Maltodextrin • Gellan gum • Lactylic esters of fatty acids • Soy lecithin • Polysorbate 60 • Soy flour • Coffee

Allergy Information: Contains MILK • WHEAT • EGGS • SOY

Consumers can see that when all the cake's sugars are combined, they become the first ingredient.

Label should show percentages by weight of key ingredients, especially those that are good or bad for your health.

Bullets separate ingredients.

Minor ingredients and allergens are listed separately.

(continued from page 60)

that destroys the cells lining the digestive system. Without these cells, the individual is not able to absorb necessary nutrients from foods.

Food Allergen Labeling

Beginning in January 2006, all manufactured foods sold in the United States must indicate on their labels if a food contains one of the eight major food allergens. The purpose of the Food Allergen Labeling and Consumer Protection Act is to allow individuals with food allergies or their parents to easily and accurately identify foods that might cause problems. The act requires that foods be clearly identified in plain English.

FOOD INTOLERANCE VS. FOOD ALLERGY

Food intolerance is a reaction to food that does not involve the immune system. Often a person cannot eat a certain food because of some metabolic defect in how his or her body processes that food. This condition may occur during digestion, or after the food is broken down and absorbed into the body. Food intolerances are more common than true food allergies, and usually, the symptoms are less severe. The extent of symptoms depends on the amount of food consumed. With an allergy, even a small amount of food can trigger symptoms. Symptoms related to food intolerance typically do not occur as quickly as those that are caused by a food allergy. Lactose intolerance is one of the most common types of food intolerance. Another is an intolerance of sulfites, a chemical that occurs naturally in some foods and wine. Sulfites may also be added to foods as a preservative. Food product labels must state if sulfites have been added.

Lactose Intolerance

Lactose is a type of sugar found only in milk. The normal digestive system produces a chemical called lactase that digests lactose into a form that the body can use. Some people are not able to produce enough lactase to digest milk. If this happens, the undigested lactose passes into the large intestine where it provides food for the many bacteria that live there. The bacteria then give off gases and irritating chemicals that lead to the symptoms of lactose intolerance. Symptoms include excessive gas, abdominal bloating or cramping, nausea, and diarrhea. Lactose intolerance is rare in infants. Among adults, it is more common among those of black, Hispanic, Asian, or Native American origin. Several steps may help an individual with lactose intolerance: drink milk only in small amounts; drink milk along with foods; see if other dairy products, such as yogurt or cheeses, can be better tolerated; buy lactose-reduced milk; take lactase pills prior to drinking milk.

REVIEW

Food allergies occur when a person's immune system responds to a food ingredient that most people can eat with no ill effects. The allergic response may range from symptoms as minor as a case of hives to a life-threatening condition called anaphylaxis. Food allergies are more common among infants and children. The foods most commonly associated with allergies are peanuts, tree nuts, eggs, milk, soybeans, fish, shellfish, and wheat. By law, foods that contain one of these eight possible allergens must clearly state its presence on the label.

4

PESTICIDES, ANTIBIOTICS, AND OTHER PROBLEMS OF FOOD PRODUCTION

L ife is not easy these days for farmers and ranchers. Their income is affected by world financial conditions as well as by the weather. Their workplaces are hazardous. And they are called on to feed an ever-growing world population. On top of these worries, a farmer's crops are subject to damage from pests of all kinds. Most farmers use chemicals to help control these pests. Cattle ranchers and poultry farmers try to raise their animals to marketable size as quickly as they can. Growth hormones and antibiotics help them accomplish this. The business of supplying agricultural chemicals to farmers and ranchers is a major U.S. industry. Therefore, it is no surprise that some of these agricultural chemicals may end up in our foods.

PESTICIDES
Why Farmers Use Pesticides

Pesticides are classified by the target they kill: herbicides are used to kill weeds, insecticides are used to kill bugs, and fungicides are used to kill fungi. U.S. farmers use more than 1 billion pounds (454 million kg) of pesticides each year. Herbicides make up the majority of pesticide use. Weed control is important because weeds compete with crops for available sun and water. If weeds are allowed to grow, crop yields are reduced. Furthermore, thousands of species of insects may reduce crop yields either by weakening a growing plant or by consuming the produce. Almost every type of crop, whether it is a grain, vegetable, or fruit, is at risk of being destroyed by some type of fungus. And sometimes, pesticides are used for nothing more than to improve the appearance of fruits or vegetables.

Unfortunately, pesticide use has not eliminated the problem of pests. Over time, weeds and insects develop resistance to a certain pesticide, or the elimination of one pest species may allow another pest species to flourish and cause just as much crop damage. Chemical companies continually develop new pesticides to keep one step ahead of the pests. Farmers may also turn to other methods, such as integrated pest management, the growth of crops with "built-in" pesticides, or organic methods.

Are Pesticides Dangerous?

With so many pesticides being applied, it is inevitable that small amounts of them remain in or on some of our foods. These small amounts of pesticides are called **residues**. A 2007 FDA monitoring program found pesticide residues in more than 60% of fruit samples. Thirty-seven percent of vegetable samples contained pesticide residues. Very few of the samples (less than 5%) contained more pesticide than the levels set as acceptable by the EPA.

Pesticides are toxic to humans as well as to plants and insects. They are capable of causing cancer, nerve system disorders, birth defects, and other diseases. But are they harmful at the very low doses that may occur on our fruits and vegetables? The EPA determines acceptable limits for pesticide residues in food. These limits are based on laboratory studies and other information for each pesticide. Sometimes, scientists or consumer groups question the safety of these limits as new information becomes available.

FIGURE 4.1 Farmer David Sarabian applies a low grade pesticide to orchard trees at his Fresno, California ranch in 2005. Although most farmers only apply pesticides that have not been banned, fruit and vegetables that have been sprayed with pesticides must be thoroughly washed before being consumed.

Because it is unethical to test potentially harmful chemicals on humans, researchers use other methods to look for links between pesticides and illness. Studies of farmworkers who apply pesticides help scientists assess the effects of exposure to high levels of pesticides. Some of these studies have revealed higher rates of Parkinson's disease, lower sperm counts, and more of certain kinds of cancer.

Urine samples of children with cancer were shown to contain higher levels of pesticides compared to healthy children. Some scientists have suggested that the currently allowable levels of some pesticides may be set too high. They are especially concerned about the health effects of these products on children, who may be eating large amounts of certain pesticide-treated foods—their developing bodies may be impacted by some of these chemicals. Also, while eating residue from a single pesticide may be reasonably safe, eating residue from several pesticides that are mixed together may be harmful.

Some pesticides may be harmful because they interfere with the body's endocrine system. The endocrine system releases chemical messengers called hormones into the bloodstream. The hormones circulate through the body to control essential functions such as growth, heart rate, and reproduction. Pesticides that interfere with hormones are called endocrine disruptors. The endocrine disruptor commonly called DDT (dichloro-diphenyl-trichloroethane), a widely recognized pesticide, was banned in the United States in 1972 because it interfered with reproduction in birds. Prior to 1972, bald eagles and other fish-eating birds accumulated DDT in their bodies from eating contaminated fish. The DDT caused their eggshells to be too thin to withstand

Endocrine System

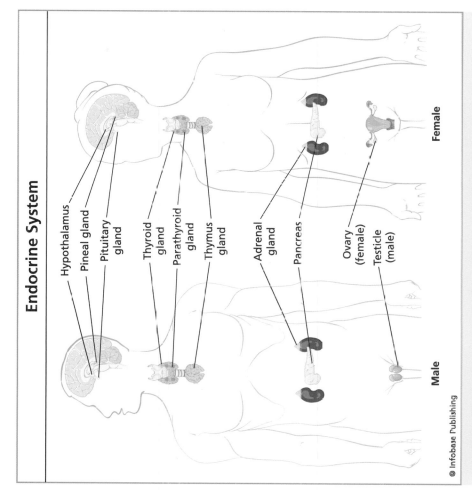

- Hypothalamus
- Pineal gland
- Pituitary gland
- Thyroid gland
- Parathyroid gland
- Thymus gland
- Adrenal gland
- Pancreas
- Ovary (female)
- Testicle (male)

Male

Female

FIGURE 4.2 Pesticides interfere with the body's endocrine system. Each of the endocrine glands produces one or more hormones.

the nesting process, so few young birds were produced. Another endocrine disruptor, **Bisphenol A** (commonly called **BPA**), is an industrial chemical used in the manufacture of plastic water

PESTICIDE FOR BREAKFAST?

Nobody gets up in the morning eager for a bowl of cereal topped with pesticides. But that is exactly what you may be getting if you top your cereal with a serving of sliced peaches. More than 90% of peaches contain pesticide residues, according to government testing. Plus, because of their soft skins, pesticides are absorbed into the peach fruit where they cannot be washed off.

FIGURE 4.3 Peaches' delicate, fuzzy skins and susceptibility to mold and pests cause them to need and retain pesticides more than many other fruits and vegetables. Although most pesticides in peaches have been found below EPA allowances, some scientists caution that low-level exposure to children and pregnant women should be monitored.

bottles and other food packaging. It has recently been detected in canned foods and infant formula.

Pesticides may accumulate in livestock from chemicals used to eliminate pests from animal holding areas. Pesticide contamination of grain fed to animals is another source of residue in meat, poultry, and dairy products.

Pesticide Regulation

"The most potent cancer-causing agent in our food supply is a substance sprayed on apples to keep them on the trees longer and make them look better." So began a 1989 report about the chemical known as Alar that was broadcast on the CBS-TV program *60 Minutes*. Almost immediately, fears of Alar contamination caused the public to grow tremendously concerned about eating apples. To allow a child to snack on a juicy red apple was suddenly perceived as being too dangerous. As a result, sales of apples fell, and the apple industry lost millions of dollars.

Although Alar is not a pesticide, it became grouped with them in the minds of the public. After the apple scare, the American public became much more aware of what they were eating. They wanted to know what chemicals were being sprayed on their foods. They especially wanted to know how these chemicals might affect their children's health. Finally, in 1996, the Food Quality Protection Act (FQPA) was passed. This new law required the EPA to take a whole new approach to regulating pesticides. It required the agency to consider the special impact of pesticides on children. All kinds of health risks had to be considered, not just cancer. Total pesticide exposure had to be considered, including that coming from nonfood sources. The FQPA also set a 10-year limit for the EPA to review the safety of all pesticides then on the market.

Currently, any new pesticide must be registered with the EPA before it is put on the market. The manufacturer must provide the EPA with all available scientific data about the new pesticide. The EPA uses the information to determine if the new pesticide is likely to affect health or the environment. Special consideration is given to any effects it might have on children. Next, the EPA decides the maximum level that is acceptable as a residue on or in food. This is called the **tolerance level**. Different tolerance levels may be set for different foods. The EPA considers public comments during the approval process. If a pesticide is approved, the EPA registration will specify the crops on which it can be used and how it can be applied. Once a pesticide is registered with the EPA, state and county agencies oversee pesticide use by local growers. While each state must follow EPA regulations, some states may actually have stricter rules about how pesticides can be used within their borders.

Once tolerance levels are set, the FDA and the USDA are responsible for monitoring food to be sure the allowed pesticide levels are not exceeded. The FDA monitors produce, fish, dairy products, and processed foods, while the USDA monitors meats, poultry, and eggs. However, it is not possible to monitor every food sold by grocery stores. Instead, the FDA selects samples of certain foods. Priority is given to those foods that are consumed in greater quantities. Each sample is tested for residues of hundreds of different pesticides. The FDA also tests for residues in a "total diet." For these tests, foods are purchased and prepared just as they would be if eaten by a typical family.

Pesticides and the Consumer

According to a senior scientist at Consumers Union, "Most uses of most pesticides on most foods do not leave residues that raise any public health concerns." Still, new findings about residues in our foods continue to make the news. Some scientists have questioned if the tolerances set by the EPA are low enough to protect the public's health. Another major concern relates to the enforcement of pesticide regulations. Every year, growers around the nation are fined for violations of pesticide restrictions. Many of these violations occur when a grower misuses an approved pesticide. When the EPA approves a pesticide, it gives clear labeling instructions regarding which crops it can be applied to and how it can be applied. The FDA and USDA, working with state agencies, serve as a final check on pesticides in our foods. But even

FIGURE 4.4 Shoppers enjoy the organic produce selection at a farmers' market in San Luis Obispo, California. The consumer push for organic fruits and vegetables is so great that a growing number of grocery stores, including the nation's largest grocery retailer, Wal-Mart, have begun offering more organic food.

their comprehensive sampling programs are able to sample only a small fraction of the foods that are produced in the United States or those foods that are imported from other countries.

Consumers also have a responsibility for dealing with pesticides. The FDA recommends some simple steps for healthful food preparation. To start with, all produce should be washed under running tap water. This applies even if the produce is to be peeled. Tough-skinned fruits and vegetables can be scrubbed with a brush. The outer leaves from leafy items such as lettuce should be removed. Since residues of pesticides may concentrate in meat fat, fatty bits should be trimmed away before the meat is cooked. This also applies to the skin and fat of poultry and fish.

Some consumers prefer to eat organic foods, which have been grown without the use of synthetic pesticides. Another option is to buy produce and meat products from local growers. This allows consumers to talk with the growers about the pesticides used on their products so they can choose accordingly.

BACTERIAL CONTAMINATION OF PRODUCE

Until recently, worries of bacterial contamination focused on meats, poultry, and dairy products. Now, it is not unusual for the source of an outbreak to be traced to some form of fresh produce, such as tomatoes, melons, or leafy greens. Changes in farming and harvesting practices have increased the risk of bacterial contamination. Workers in the fields may begin the preparation for shipping, for example stripping away outer lettuce leaves. This handling of produce in the absence of hand-washing facilities may spread bacteria. Consumer demand has resulted in new products like chopped and bagged lettuce. This additional handling creates new opportunities for the introduction of contaminants into food. Even bagged lettuce labeled as "prewashed" has been found to contain bacteria that may come from sewage contamination. Some farmers now use mechanized harvesting in an attempt to provide consumers with fresh produce at a lower cost. These giant machines may scoop up bits of soil, along with bacterial contamination, as they move down the rows of vegetables.

ANTIBIOTICS IN MEAT AND DAIRY PRODUCTS

Picture a peaceful rural scene in which a contented cow grazes happily in a lush green pasture. As pretty as this picture may be, there is something not quite accurate about it. The fact is, most of the cattle raised for beef production today do not live this luxurious lifestyle. Modern ranching methods force animals to spend much of their lives crowded together in small areas called Concentrated Animal Feeding Operations (CAFOs). CAFOs have the advantage of quickly and efficiently getting more meat to the marketplace. However, they have the disadvantage of serving as prime breeding grounds for animal diseases. In response, CAFO operators use antibiotics both to treat and to prevent disease in farm animals. These changes in livestock practices have led to concerns about the effect of these antibiotics on our food supplies and on human health.

Following the discovery of penicillin by Sir Alexander Fleming in 1928, antibiotics were hailed as miracle drugs. Since they became available for patient use in 1944, they have saved countless lives. Today, the use of antibiotics to treat infectious diseases is so commonplace that we tend to take them for granted. Antibiotics can kill bacteria that cause diseases such as pneumonia, tuberculosis, or strep throat. Before antibiotics, people routinely died of these dreaded diseases. It did not take long for farmers to realize that these miracle drugs could also be used to treat their sick animals. By happy coincidence, farmers observed that animals treated with antibiotics gained weight faster. And the faster the weight gain, the sooner a product like beefsteak could arrive at the supermarket.

It is now routine practice to add small doses of antibiotics to the feed of healthy farm animals. These small doses given to healthy animals are called subtherapeutic doses. A sick animal is treated with a larger therapeutic dose. Many of the antibiotics given to animals are almost identical to the antibiotics used to treat humans. Doctors have warned that the continued use of subtherapeutic doses of antibiotics in animals will lead to loss of effectiveness of these antibiotics in humans.

Treating a disease with antibiotics is not a one-size-fits-all treatment. Each type of antibiotic has its own method of attacking bacterial cells. One antibiotic may interfere with the bacterial cell's chemical processes of producing proteins, while another may cause the cell wall to break down, causing the cell to die. When a person becomes infected with a bacterial disease, a doctor will prescribe the appropriate antibiotic to kill the invading bacteria. This is why doctors sometimes want to take a sample swab from a sore throat to determine the type of bacterial invaders. Then they can match the best antibiotic treatment to that particular invader.

Each time a colony of bacteria is exposed to antibiotics, there is a chance that a few bacteria will be resistant to the antibiotic

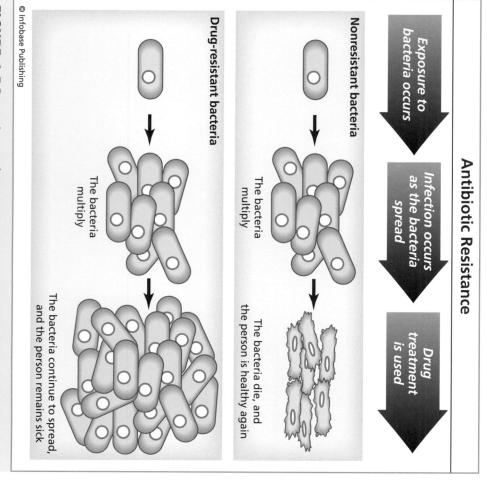

Antibiotic Resistance

Exposure to bacteria occurs

Infection occurs as the bacteria spread

Drug treatment is used

Nonresistant bacteria

The bacteria multiply

The bacteria die, and the person is healthy again

Drug-resistant bacteria

The bacteria multiply

The bacteria continue to spread, and the person remains sick

FIGURE 4.5 Bacteria can become resistant to antibiotics when the antibiotics are used repeatedly to combat them over time.

effects. This is due to the constant small genetic changes that bacteria undergo as they multiply into new bacterial cells. Occasionally, one of these genetic changes will produce a cell that is able to fight back against an antibiotic's method of attack. If this one cell rapidly multiplies, the antibiotic may not be able to help an infected person fight off the infection.

The same process occurs when animals are given antibiotics. A few antibiotic-resistant bacteria may develop. These bacteria may then be transferred from the feces of these animals to the air of their confined spaces or to the water runoff from feedlots. Produce could be accidentally contaminated because of leakage from waste ponds. The meat produced from these animals may also be contaminated with bacteria. Should someone become infected by eating food contaminated with a strain of antibiotic-resistant bacteria, the treatment options are limited. An otherwise minor foodborne illness could quickly get out of control.

The case of fluoroquinolone use in poultry is an example of why the medical community is concerned about the overuse of antibiotics. Fluoroquinolones (such as Cipro) are a class of powerful antibiotics that became available in the 1980s. They are active against a wide range of disease-causing bacteria and are particularly important for treating severe cases of foodborne illness. In 1995, the FDA approved fluoroquinolones for use in poultry. Within a short time, more people began to be diagnosed with fluoroquinolone-resistant *Campylobacter* infection from eating contaminated poultry. In 2000, the FDA proposed a ban on fluoroquinolone use in poultry. The ban was opposed by the manufacturer of the drug, but it finally took effect in 2005 after a lengthy court battle. This marked the first time an animal drug was banned over concern about the effect of antibiotic resistance on human health.

HORMONES IN MEAT AND DAIRY PRODUCTS

Ranchers routinely inject young beef cattle with hormones to increase their growth rate. Natural male or female sex hormones help animals grow to maturity faster and increase their muscle mass for meat production. The hormones are generally injected in pellet form under the ear skin because the ear does not enter the food supply. Using hormones to speed growth rate reduces beef production costs. These savings can then be passed on to consumers in the form of lower meat prices.

Dairy farmers use several methods to increase their milk production of their cows. One of the most common is the use of a genetically engineered growth hormone, called **recombinant bovine growth hormone (rBGH)**. The use of rBGH in cattle has been controversial since the FDA approved the hormone in 1993. Those in favor of rBGH use note that the hormone is unlike any human hormone, and that it is broken down in the human digestive tract, making it biologically inactive. Cows treated with rBGH also produce larger amounts of an insulin-like growth hormone, which is a natural human hormone. Plus, rBGH-treated cows tend to get more infections and thus must receive more antibiotics. Part of the rBGH controversy deals with whether milk should be labeled to indicate it is from rBGH-treated cows. Those opposed to labeling note it is not possible to tell the difference in milk from rBGH-treated cows, since all cow milk contains some natural growth hormone.

Because hormones are naturally occurring chemicals, they are always present in meat and dairy products whether or not the animal source has been treated with hormones. Because of this, it is not possible to test for hormone residues in the same way that sample monitoring is used to test for pesticides. So far, however, studies have not conclusively linked human illness to consumption of meat or dairy products from hormone-treated cattle. Nevertheless, many consumers worry about eating meat or drinking milk from cattle that have been treated with hormones. European Union countries do not allow the use of hormones in cattle and do not allow imported meats from such cattle. Major U.S. stores, such as Wal-Mart and Starbucks, only sell milk from dairies that have pledged not to use rBGH.

CONTAMINATION FROM AIR AND WATER

Many industrial chemicals are released into the environment through the air and water. Some of these remain in the environment for a long time and may eventually find their way into our food supply. Sometimes, a pesticide may be banned but will remain in the soil for years. Plants grown in contaminated soil or fish taken from contaminated water may sometimes contain pesticide residues. Cattle may graze on grass that has been contaminated with airborne pollutants. Some chemicals may reach shallow coastal waters where they are taken up by shellfish. Fish in inland lakes can accumulate chemicals dissolved in the water.

Mercury is one of the air pollutants released by coal-fired power plants. Much of it ends up in lakes and streams where it is converted by bacterial action into a form called methylmercury. This form of mercury is a potent toxin to the human nervous system. As bigger fish eat smaller contaminated fish, the toxin moves up the food chain and becomes more concentrated. Eating fish contaminated with methylmercury does not result in obvious food poisoning. However, fairly small doses can interfere with a developing fetus. For this reason, pregnant women are warned

WHAT DROVE THE MAD HATTER MAD?

The Mad Hatter character in Lewis Carroll's *Alice's Adventures in Wonderland* may owe his name to mercury poisoning. Workers in the hat industry of the 1800s were exposed to high levels of mercury used in the hat-making process. Many of them developed symptoms of mercury poisoning, such as confused speech, hallucinations, and other signs of "madness." Eventually, the expression "mad as a hatter" became a figure of speech. It is thought that Lewis Carroll's awareness of hatters who were suffering from mercury poisoning inspired him in creating the odd behavior of the Mad Hatter.

to be cautious about the amount of fish they eat. A study by the CDC found that nearly 1 in 10 women and children had mercury in their bodies at close to toxic levels.

Polychlorinated biphenyl (PCB) is a long-lasting chemical that is used in industrial applications. Its use has been banned in the United States since 1977. However, it is still present in items such as electrical transformers that were manufactured before that time. Some PCB contamination of soil and water persists long after the ban. PCB residues may still be found in fish or animal fat, where they have become concentrated as they worked their way up the food chain.

REVIEW

Modern farming and ranching methods rely on the use of chemicals, some of which may remain as residues on or in foods. Pesticides, which are used to protect crops from weeds, insects, and other pests, are also toxic to humans. The EPA sets a food residue tolerance level for each pesticide at an amount determined not to be a danger to health. These levels are enforced by sampling and testing food products, but it is not possible to sample more than a small fraction of the foods that make up the American diet. Also, there is disagreement on the levels of these chemicals that may be dangerous to human health. The administration of antibiotics to livestock poses the danger of antibiotic-resistant bacteria that could contaminate the food supply and cause human infections that are difficult to treat. Some long-lasting industrial chemicals end up as pollution in air, water, and soil, where they can be taken up by plants, livestock, or fish that become part of the human food supply.

5

FOOD PROCESSING AND PREPARATION

At one time, the processing of a family's evening meal might have started with grabbing a chicken from the farmyard and plucking its feathers before throwing it in the stew pot. But the chicken we buy at the grocery store today is the end result of a huge industrial chain. It begins with the grain and chemical industries that support large-scale poultry facilities and ends with the advertising that attracts shoppers into the grocery store. For the chicken that we buy in the form of "nuggets," food scientists, food processing machinery, and lots of food additives are also in the mix. When that chicken arrives on the dinner table, it has already had a long and checkered history that some people may not find so appetizing.

BACKGROUND OF FOOD PROCESSING

In the 1800s, women who lived in rural areas knew all about food and food quality. They could tell with a glance or a touch if a chicken was tender or if berries were ready for jam-making. Even women who did not have a vegetable garden of their own to tend knew how to recognize the quality of the foods at their corner grocer or butcher. By using sight and smell, they could tell if food was fresh, wholesome, and tasty. They also knew how to process foods so they would keep all year long. They made pickles, home-canned fruits, sourdough bread, sausages, smoked meats, yogurt, and cheeses. These processes not only preserved the foods, but in most cases, made them more nutritious and tasty. Imagine the dilemma a housewife faced when she was first offered the opportunity to buy vegetables packed into a tin can!

Soldiers and sailors were the first to eat canned foods, not by choice but by necessity. Several canneries sprang up during the U.S. Civil War (1861–1865) for the purpose of providing food for the troops on a large scale. In the decades following the war, those canneries sought new markets for their products. They needed to look no further than the fast-growing U.S. cities, which were crammed with folks who had recently arrived from the farm. Housewives living in apartment buildings had no land to grow a vegetable garden, and there was no place for them to process and store their own foods for the winter. With that in mind, all the canneries had to do was sell them on the idea of feeding their families food from a can.

Early canned foods were not of very good quality. Most of them were overcooked, and the canning process changed their color, flavor, and texture. Canners were still working out the kinks in their processing methods. When one unfortunate woman opened a can of molasses, "the lid was thrown aside and something shot out like the shot of a gun and struck her full force in the left eye." There were occasional cases of botulism because the canners did not yet understand the necessity of processing foods at high temperatures to destroy bacteria. The canners tried to compensate for their foods' shortcomings with appealing can labels. Most of these labels featured pretty rural scenes and perhaps a luscious-looking vegetable unlike what was contained inside the can.

FOOD DECEPTION: IT IS NOTHING NEW

Since their beginnings, food manufacturers have always been searching for new products to attract grocery shoppers. Back in 1873, the new product was oleomargarine: Beef fat left over from the slaughterhouses was cleaned and minced, mixed with hog fat, salted, and dyed. It might look like butter, but the flavor did not compare. Still, it could be sold at a cheaper price, and the unsuspecting consumer could be confused by the labels. Some makers called the new product "butterine" or even "BUTTER-ine." One maker claimed his product was "churned especially for lovers of good butter."

The new product made dairymen suffer a loss of business. In response, they took their cause to the U.S. Congress where lawmakers debated the issue for 13 days. The dairy industry claimed oleomargarine came from diseased animals and contained poisonous additives. One government official warned of bad effects on public health from such a radical change in a common food item. Oleomargarine makers countered that their manufacturing process was more sanitary than a dairy barn. The fight over oleomargarine was one of the earliest clashes between traditional food production and the food-processing industry. Similar controversies continue to this day.

INFLUENCES ON CONSUMERS
Appealing to Our Taste Buds

Everyone likes to eat foods that taste good. So, why do we all like different foods? As with other human traits, our taste preferences are influenced by genetics. Our preferences have their origins in ancient people who relied on their sense of taste for survival. Those who had access to sweet-tasting foods had a readily available and nutritious diet. Foods that tasted bitter were likely to be spoiled or contain toxic substances. The inherited ability to taste bitterness gave people an advantage over those less able to recognize foods they should not eat. And the taste of fats was welcome because fats provided a much-needed calorie source for people who survived by their ability to hunt and trap animals.

The sense of taste is activated by receptor cells located in the thousands of taste buds on the tongue. These chemical changes are transmitted to the brain, where humans perceive them as tasting good or not tasting good. The sense of smell also affects taste preferences and is made up of a separate set of receptors in the nasal passages. But our taste preferences are much more than the set of chemical receptors and number of taste buds that we were born with. The brain's taste detection system is also affected by our life experiences. People generally prefer the foods they grew up eating, or foods with which they have some pleasant association. Sometimes, a strong dislike of a certain food has its origins in a bad experience, such as a food eaten before or during an illness. Aroma also plays a role in whether or not a food appeals to us. Memories we associate with certain smells play a big role in shaping our food preferences.

Despite individual preferences, the vast majority of people enjoy eating foods that are salty, fatty, or sweet. Food processors know that increasing one or more of these flavors in a manufactured food product makes it more appealing to consumer taste buds. These additions are inexpensive and not harmful in small amounts. But sometimes foods contain a surprising amount of these ingredients without the consumer knowing it. For example, the average American eats twice the recommended amount of sodium (salt), and 75% of this comes from processed foods. Sugar in processed foods increases calorie intake with no nutritive value—a can of soda may contain more than 10 teaspoons (about 5 milliliters) of sugar. Fats are much higher in calories than either carbohydrates or proteins. They also make foods more appealing because they add taste and texture.

The food industry introduces thousands of new manufactured products into the marketplace every year. Many of these (with some recent entries including brand names such as Cakesters, Chicken Wyngs, and Quorn) bear little relation to

FUNGI ON THE MENU?

If you are among the millions of Americans who choose to eat less meat for health or environmental reasons, you may have already tried eating a Quorn patty. Many of those who have tried it say it tastes like chicken, with a nice texture that is similar to lean meat. Nutritionally, it is a good source of protein and fiber, and healthier than meat because of its low fat content.

Quorn is a manufactured meat substitute produced from a soil fungus, *Fusarium venenatum*. This fungus was discovered growing in the soil of an English field. Its potential as an efficient protein source was recognized by food-scientist developers in the 1960s. The manufacturing process consists of culturing the fungi in a large vat, which eventually results in a fibrous high-protein doughy substance. The resulting product, along with flavorings, oils, salt, and other ingredients, is then texturized, shaped, and packaged as various products such as "chicken" patties and "turkey" roasts.

Quorn products have been approved for sale by the FDA under the category of foods "generally recognized as safe." They are available in the freezer section of many grocery stores. The consumer group Center for Science in the Public Interest (CSPI), however, objects to the sale of Quorn products. They note the large number of reports from people who have gotten sick after eating Quorn, and consider it an issue of food safety on the order of peanut or shellfish allergies. According to a CSPI spokesman, "Quorn Foods should either find a fungus that doesn't make people sick, or place prominent warning labels about the vomiting, diarrhea, breathing difficulties, and other symptoms Quorn causes in some consumers."

Like other products made by the food-processing industry, Quorn is not found growing on a farm. It is a good source of protein and can be produced with little environmental impact. However, some consumers may feel unsure about what they are eating or how healthy it might be.

any natural food found on a farm. For consumers who are concerned about eating too much sugar or too many calories, food manufacturers have developed chemical alternatives to their natural sources. Package labels of processed foods may have long lists of unfamiliar substances that are added to appeal to our taste buds. Although these substances have been tested by their makers and approved by the FDA, the label information is present to help consumers make informed choices about what they eat.

Make It Fast and Make It Cheap

By most measures, the food we buy is a bargain. Americans spend less than 10% of their incomes on food, much less than was spent in previous decades. Over time, farmers and food manufacturers have learned how to produce food more efficiently and economically. Some of these savings are passed on to consumers. However, the example of ground beef tells us that these economies do not always add up to a good bargain. Meat producers buy scrap meats cheaply from several sources and mix these to produce hamburger patties at a much lower cost compared to the local butcher who grinds up a piece of beef himself. Yet the processed hamburger patties have a much greater chance of being contaminated with *E. coli* O157:H7.

Food additives may be used as a substitute for real foods. For example, red food dye and flavoring may replace cherries in a snack food. While most of these food additives are perfectly safe to eat, a few of them have the potential to cause allergies. Also, some of them have been inadequately tested for their effects on health, according to consumer groups. Most shoppers would probably prefer having real fruit in their snack, but they would have to choose between that more expensive snack and paying a lower price for the one that contains additives.

Many busy families have little time to prepare nutritious meals for themselves. Even people who know that eating fresh, locally grown produce is the safest and healthiest choice may not have the time for necessary shopping and food preparation. Food processors have responded to changing family needs by devising a huge array of convenience foods and prepared foods. Some of these consumer choices may involve compromising food safety, for example, if prepared foods are not kept at proper temperatures. Convenience foods require the addition of chemical preservatives to increase their shelf life.

MEAT PROCESSING

Fresh packaged meats are by their nature different from other processed foods. Since they are derived from living animals, there is not an expectation that they will be completely free of microorganisms. The concern for consumers lies in the extent of the contamination and if the organisms are among the rare strains that present a serious threat to human health. Even a century after revelations regarding the processes described in Sinclair's novel, *The Jungle*, slaughterhouses remain messy, dirty places. However, recent innovations in the meat industry are aimed at making their products safer for consumers: pathogen testing, science-based control systems, worker education, and improved equipment. In addition to processing improvements, USDA inspectors provide a check on the system in order to reduce the threat of foodborne illnesses.

Despite all these efforts, thousands of pounds of meats are recalled each year because of the possibility of pathogen contamination. In one innovative process, finely ground beef trimmings are treated with ammonia gas to kill hazardous *E. coli* and *Salmonella* bacteria. These trimmings are the parts of cattle most likely to become contaminated with fecal matter as they move through the slaughterhouse. Formerly, they were mostly used for pet food or for lard. The ground-up trimmings, described as "pink slime" by one government employee, are combined with ground beef to produce hamburger patties. These manufactured patties have become a staple hamburger source served by major fast-food chains and school lunch pro-

(continues on page 90)

THE NOVEL THAT PRODDED CONGRESS

There would be meat stored in great piles in rooms; and the water from leaky roofs would drip over it, and thousands of rats would race about on it . . . the meat would be shoveled into carts, and the man who did the shoveling would not trouble to lift out a rat even when he saw one—there were things that went into the sausage in comparison with which a poisoned rat was a tidbit.

—Upton Sinclair, *The Jungle* (1906)

By the early 1900s, a few powerful corporations controlled the meatpacking business. Operations were centered in a few cities, with Chicago being the largest. Mass production methods and workers on assembly lines enabled a single plant to process thousands of animals. Because of their size, the corporations were able to exert control over the ranchers who produced the animals, the employees who worked in their plants, the consumers who purchased their products, and elected officials who passed the laws. In Chicago, stockyards with herds of recently arrived cattle, huge factory buildings that served as slaughterhouses, refrigerated railroad cars to carry off fresh meats to butcher shops all over the country, and housing for the factory workers were all crowded into a neighborhood called Packingtown.

Upton Sinclair was an ambitious young writer with little knowledge of the meatpacking industry. When an editor suggested that the industry might make a good subject for a novel, Sinclair headed to Packingtown. There, he spent seven weeks researching the industry, interviewing workers and observing the appalling conditions inside the plants. Sinclair's fictionalized account described how injured, diseased, or even dead animals were slipped past government inspectors; how spoiled meats were treated with chemicals to hide their taste; and even episodes in which workers fell into the lard vats and went unnoticed until there was nothing left to be fished out but their bones. The worst of the scrap meats were ground up with spices and put into cans to be sold as "potted chicken" or "deviled ham."

The fictional plant was owned by "a man who was trying to make as much money out of it as he could, and did not care in the least how he did it."

The Jungle quickly became a best seller when it was published in 1906. The public was outraged when they learned about the filthy and mislabeled meats, and they let their elected officials hear about it. President Theodore Roosevelt got so many letters that he appointed a special commission to investigate the Chicago meatpackers. Their report confirmed the accuracy of Sinclair's descriptions—President Roosevelt himself described the conditions as "revolting." Despite strong opposition from the meatpacking industry, Congress responded to the public outcry and passed the Meat Inspection Act of 1906.

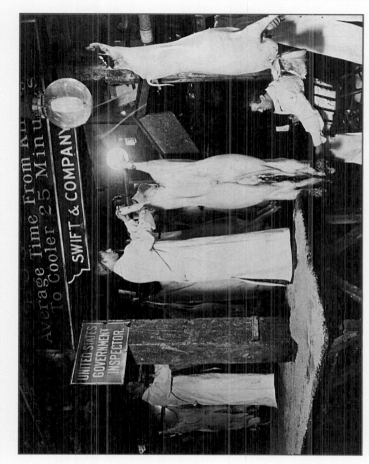

FIGURE 5.1 Meat inspectors examine hog carcasses hanging at the Swift & Company packinghouse in Chicago, circa 1900.

(continued from page 87)

grams. Even after school cooks complained about the smell of ammonia in the raw meat, the hamburger was approved for use because it reduced costs by about three cents per pound. Although producers claimed that ammonia-treated meat would not contain pathogens, government testing has revealed several incidents of bacterial contamination.

FOOD ADDITIVES
Why Food Processors Use Additives

How tasty would a pretzel be without salt? Pumpkin pie without cinnamon? Oleomargarine without yellow coloring? Cooks have been preserving our foods and whetting our appetites with food additives for thousands of years. Modern food manufacturers use additives for many of the same reasons. The difference today is that they just have a lot more ingredients to choose from.

Many food additives act as preservatives against the effects of air, molds, bacteria, or fungi. Antioxidants are commonly added to foods that contain fats to prevent them from developing an off-flavor. (Antioxidants that often appear on food labels are known as BHA and BHT) Vitamin C acts as an antioxidant and is also beneficial to health. Calcium propionate is added to bread to prevent molds. Sodium nitrites are added to cured meats, such as sausage and bacon.

Vitamins, minerals, and fiber are added to foods to make them more nutritious. Sometimes vitamins are added to processed fruits and vegetables to replace those that are lost during processing. Fortified cereals have vitamins and minerals added in order to provide an extra source of these natural and essential nutrients. Sometimes, essential nutrients are added to certain foods as a way to prevent diseases that are caused by nutrient deficiency. During the 1930s, rickets, a disease that affects the bones and is caused by a vitamin D deficiency, was a serious public health problem.

A program to fortify milk with vitamin D virtually eliminated rickets. Today, most of the U.S. milk supply is fortified with vitamin D.

Many foods are improved by the addition of sweeteners, spices, color, or flavorings. Often, these additives enhance the natural flavors of foods. A color additive might restore fruit or vegetable color that has been lost in processing. New food products require additives to give them the consistency and texture of foods we are used to eating. Cereal manufacturers know that Americans like their cereals crunchy, so they devise additives that will give a cereal longer "bowl life" (the time it takes cereal to get soggy in a bowl of milk). Thickening agents help to keep mixes of oils, liquids, and solids well mixed. Some additives are chemicals that occur naturally in foods, and some may be chemical copies of natural substances. Artificial ingredients are

LOOKING FOR DIRTY BIRDS

Consumers Union, the independent consumer testing group that publishes the magazine *Consumer Reports*, regularly tests store-bought chickens for the presence of *Salmonella* and *Campylobacter*. Unfortunately, their tests continue to find many of the chickens contaminated with one or the other of these bacteria. Each year, thousands of Americans are hospitalized with infections caused by eating foods contaminated with these organisms. Poultry farmers attempt to reduce the presence of the bacteria by practicing good sanitation in their poultry houses. Even so, many birds arrive at processing plants with bacterial contamination. Poultry processors have developed new processing equipment and bacteria-removal processes in order to reduce the risk of these bacteria remaining in chickens when they are shipped to grocery stores. The USDA testing program is also helping to find where problems exist and how improvements can be made in order to protect public health.

those that do not occur in nature and are made using chemical processes.

Regulating Food Additive Safety

The FDA has primary responsibility for testing and monitoring the safety of food additives. Any new food additive, or new use of an already approved additive, must first be submitted to the FDA for approval. The manufacturer must provide evidence that the substance is safe for human consumption in the way it is proposed for use. The FDA reviews the properties of the substance, its possible short- and long-term effects on human health, the amount of the substance that is likely to be consumed, and other safety factors. Regulators at the USDA are also consulted if an additive is proposed for use in meat products. If FDA approval is given, the regulation will specify the amount of the substance that can be added to a food. This level is set at a much lower level by the FDA than the amount that might cause any effect on health. This provides a built-in safety margin.

There are certain additives that do not have to go through the FDA approval process. When the U.S. Congress passed food additive laws in 1958, it was decided that certain additives did not have to be reviewed by the FDA. These were substances that had a long history of safe use in foods, such as salt, sugar, vitamins, and spices. Also, they were regarded as safe for human health by qualified scientists. Food additives on this list are referred to in the food industry as **Generally Recognized As Safe (GRAS)**. However, the FDA can still regulate GRAS substances, for example, if new scientific information indicates a safety issue concerning a substance or if a new use of the substance, is proposed.

CONSUMER CONCERNS
Nutrition

Much of the industrial processing of natural foods destroys nutrients. The milling of wheat grains presents a good example of how this happens. At it goes through the mill, wheat is crushed, sifted, and separated, removing the germ and bran from the starchy interior. Many people prefer bakery products that are made from this starchy white interior, or white flour. The food industry also prefers white flour because of its longer shelf life. Unfortunately, white flour has hardly any fiber, vitamins, or minerals, which are found in the bran and germ that has been removed from the wheat grain.

Similarly, cooking vegetables results in a loss of vitamins, even when fresh vegetables are cooked at home. Typically, commercially processed vegetables are cooked at higher temperatures for longer times, which destroys even more vitamins. Fruits and vegetables contain much of their nutrient value in their skins. These skins are almost always removed in food processing. When fresh vegetables are not available, frozen vegetables are a better choice than canned because they retain higher nutrient values.

Grilled Meats

The grilling of meats at high temperatures converts natural substances in the meat to chemicals called **heterocyclic amines,** or HCAs. These compounds are capable of causing cancer in laboratory animals. It is not known if HCAs can cause cancer in humans in the amounts that might be present on grilled meats. While it is important to grill meats to the recommended internal temperatures to protect against food poisoning, high grilling temperatures can cause excessive charring. For those wishing to reduce their intake of HCAs while still enjoying grilled meats, several steps are recommended: Precook meat briefly in the microwave, and pat it dry before grilling; cook at a lower surface temperature (but to same internal temperature); use marinades; and do not cook directly over flames.

Labeling

Food manufacturers are required by law to list all product ingredients on the label. They are listed in order of the amount of the ingredient present in the product. Yet these lists can be bewildering for the consumer because many ingredients have unfamiliar chemical names. Some color additives must be listed and are given code names such as "yellow 5." The FDA has designated certain color additives that can be listed only as "artificial colors." Some ingredients can be grouped together and listed only as "flavors," "spices," or "artificial flavoring." Certain allergenic ingredients have been designated for special listing. A food label is also an opportunity for last-minute advertising at the point of purchase. Bold letters on package fronts may proclaim "farm fresh," "no chemicals," or "natural." Such terms are not well defined, and they can cause great confusion for consumers who are attempting to select safe and nutritious foods. Guidelines to require more accurate front-of-label information could help consumers to make more healthful food choices.

Chemical Testing

The FDA maintains a list of "everything added to food" in the United States. The list has more than 3,000 entries, and there are other legal substances that are not included on the list. No wonder the average American diet includes hundreds of chemicals. All of them have been tested, either by long-term use in the human diet, or by laboratory methods and other information. Many new chemical additives are first tested on animals to be sure there are no harmful effects. Some scientists and parent organizations have raised questions about the adequacy of testing for certain chemicals. Questions remain about the amounts of some additives that can be eaten safely or the health impacts of eating so many chemicals. Also, it is not really possible to test the body's long-term tolerances of added chemicals.

BPA in Packaging

Advances in food packaging have accompanied other advances in the food industry. Food packaging helps to preserve foods and often adds to the convenience of serving or storing foods. The ready availability of all kinds of plastics has brought about big changes in how foods are packaged. Bisphenol A (BPA) is a chemical building block that is used to make polycarbonate plastic, a tough and lightweight plastic with many uses. It is used to make clear plastic food containers and water bottles that are heat-resistant and durable. BPA is also found in epoxy resins. The resins are used as protective liners for food and beverage cans. These tough and chemical resistant linings help to maintain the quality of the can's contents.

BPA is also found inside almost every person. During 2003 to 2004, the CDC took urine samples from more than 2,000 people to test for the presence of BPA. The tests found BPA in 93% of samples from people age six and older. Although these people had BPA present in their bodies, there was no suggestion that levels of BPA were high enough to cause health risks. According to the CDC, human exposure to BPA occurs through our diet. BPA leaches from can liners and polycarbonate bottles into our foods and drinks. The FDA has tested the safety of BPA as used in food packaging and has concluded that foods in packages containing BPA are safe for human consumption. However, because BPA is in such widespread use, and because of rising public concern about this, the safety of BPA is being reevaluated. Laboratory animal studies have linked BPA to reproductive problems, abnormal fetal development, early puberty in females, and cancer. Scientists at the National Toxicology Program of the U.S. National Institutes of Health have indicated concerns about the impact of BPA exposure on fetuses, infants, and children. While scientists continue to study the evidence about BPA, consumers who wish to avoid BPA can take several steps: Reduce the use of canned foods; use infant formula bottles labeled BPA-free; avoid putting plastic containers in the dishwasher; avoid using plastic containers for warming foods in a microwave; use glass or stainless-steel containers, particularly for hot food and liquids.

RESTAURANT DINING

"Slime in the Ice Machine!" "Cockroaches in the Kitchen!" Attention-grabbing reports like these appear often on the evening TV news. Yet the truth is that there are even more important food safety concerns at local restaurants. Many busy families rely on

FIGURE 5.2 A Sherman Oaks, California, restaurant displays an "A" health inspection grade in March 2010. The boards of health in a growing number of U.S. cities are requiring restaurants to post grades given by inspectors at the entrance to their eateries.

restaurant meals, either eat-in or take-out, several times each week. By some estimates, these meals also account for more than half of U.S. cases of foodborne illnesses.

All public food service establishments are regularly inspected by local public health departments to be sure they are following proper safety procedures. The most serious violations are for improper food holding temperatures, poor employee hygiene, unsafe food sources, improper cooking times or temperatures, and contaminated food contact surfaces. As we have learned earlier, each of these practices can lead to the spread of foodborne illnesses. In a restaurant serving hundreds of meals every day, there is the potential to quickly spread infection throughout a community.

Unfortunately, the average restaurant diner has little way of knowing if a particular restaurant has been guilty of violations or if steps have been taken to correct the violations. Results of health inspections are often not readily available. One reporting system now used in a few cities has proved effective in reducing illnesses caused by contaminated restaurant food. In this system, the restaurant is given a grade—either A, B, or C—following its annual inspection, and the result is clearly posted on the front of the restaurant. Who would choose to eat food from a restaurant with "C," the poorest safety grade, posted on its front window? This system of public posting provides real incentive for restaurants to adhere to proper safety procedures.

REVIEW

Thanks to the modern food-processing industry, most Americans have ready access to a wholesome and varied selection of foods. But demands on food processors have occasionally led to deceptive practices and cost-cutting methods that compromise food safety. Consumer demands for processed and ready-to-eat foods have led to increased use of food additives. New food additives undergo scientific review by the FDA to assess health effects prior to approval. Fresh meat products are particularly susceptible to bacterial contamination because of the possibility of fecal contamination during butchering. As more is known about the effects of chemicals on the human body, new concerns have emerged about sources of chemical contamination during food storage or preparation. Restaurant food accounts for a large portion of foodborne illnesses. Although restaurants are regularly inspected by local public health agencies, this information may or may not be readily available as a guide for consumers.

6

GENETICALLY MODIFIED FOODS

Many Americans have concerns about the safety of genetically modified foods and prefer not to eat them. Yet most people eat them unknowingly in processed foods. Corn chips may contain genetically modified corn. Among other foods, sodas may contain high-fructose corn syrup from genetically modified corn; canola oil, a common food ingredient, likely came from genetically modified plants. European countries severely restrict the sale of genetically modified foods. Some African countries have turned down food aid because it came from genetically modified plants. So why is there all this controversy? And are genetically modified foods safe to eat?

FOOD AND BIOLOGY BEFORE THE GENETIC AGE

Biotechnology means the use of biological organisms or biological processes to make or change livings things. It has been used to improve our foods since long before anyone knew about genetics. For example, a biological accident may have produced the first cheese thousands of years ago. Somehow, milk wound up being stored in a cow stomach so long that it absorbed a protein called rennet that comes from the cow's stomach lining. Someone noticed that a tasty product resulted after storage and that product was what we know as cheese. The many cheeses we enjoy today rely on a biological process that causes milk to curdle. Similarly, beer and wine are produced by yeast fermentation processes that were discovered long ago. And bread, the "staff of life," depends on the action of yeast for its nice, light texture. No one questions the safety of these processes. Their value has been established by long experience.

Farmers have used biotechnology since the beginnings of agriculture. The biological process of selective breeding has allowed them to improve their animals and crops over time. Dairy farmers breed those cows that produce the most milk, increasing the chance that the offspring will also be good producers. By saving seeds from the largest vegetables to sow in next year's garden, the garden's harvest will increase over time. Sometimes, a farmer may want to combine two desirable plant traits in a single plant. A plant having a desirable trait can be crossed with a plant having a second desirable trait by carefully controlling pollination. The technical name for this process is hybridization. Over many years, selective breeding has led to better crop yields, tastier fruits, and more milk production. Rice breeders in China have produced hybrid rice that increases crop yields by 30%. In Africa, new varieties of corn can withstand drought.

Even so, a drawback of selective breeding is that it is not completely controllable. From time to time, undesirable traits also occur due to the mixing of traits from the parent plants or animals. Plus, trait selection is limited to those traits that currently exist in the plant or animal species. Some people view genetic modification as a harmless extension of natural selective-breeding processes. Others consider it a radical departure that has introduced hazards into our food supply.

FIGURE 6.1 Seed researcher David Joynt of R&D Agriculture looks at female hybrid broccoli that he patented with flowering male broccoli (in the background) in Salinas, California, in 2004. Joynt, along with fellow researcher Robert Barham, has also developed broccoli that can thrive in sweltering temperatures above 80°F (27°C), as opposed to its typical 40°F (4°C) to 70°F (21°C).

HOW GENETIC MODIFICATION WORKS

Many people enjoy corn on the cob dripping with butter on a July day and the spicy aroma of a pumpkin pie made from the autumn pumpkin crop. Fortunately, we can enjoy these treats without thinking too much about the science that brought them to us. But what made that corn plant produce ears of corn in July? Why do pumpkin vines produce those beautiful orange treats in October? Buried within seeds planted by farmers in the spring were the genetic codes specific to the type of plant. That same code was duplicated in every cell, and this genetic information controlled plant growth to produce the farmer's crop during certain seasons of the year.

The genetic code is essentially a long series of chemical messages lined up in a molecule of **deoxyribonucleic acid (DNA)**. DNA molecules are tightly coiled into structures called **chromosomes**. Every variety of plant or animal has a characteristic number of paired chromosomes. For example, cells of corn plants contain 10 pairs of chromosomes. **Genes** are segments of chromosomes that include the chemical codes for certain traits of the plant or animal. Genes for a given trait come in pairs. One member of each pair is inherited from each of an individual's parents. A particular gene is always found at the same location of a specific chromosome.

The field of genetic engineering has grown rapidly in recent decades. Scientists now know the location of genes in the DNA of many organisms, including bacteria, corn plants, and humans. For example, a gene on chromosome 4 of corn DNA makes sweet corn taste sweet. They have discovered tools that act like tiny scissors, called *restriction enzymes*, to snip out certain genes. A chemical that acts like a genetic glue, *ligase*, can be used to paste another gene into the location.

Genetic Engineering

Some of the greatest discoveries of the twenty-first century are taking place on a miniature scale. Scientists are hard at work mapping out the genes hidden within the cells of all kinds of

Genetic Engineering for Plants

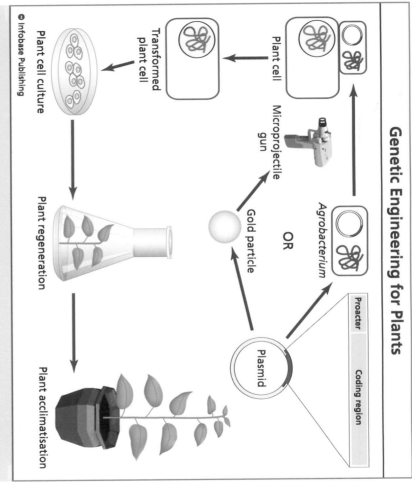

Plant cell

Microprojectile gun

Agrobacterium

OR

Gold particle

Plasmid

Proacter | Coding region

Transformed plant cell

Plant cell culture

Plant regeneration

Plant acclimatisation

© Infobase Publishing

FIGURE 6.2 Genetically modified plants contain one or more genes of another species. The newly introduced traits may make the plant resistant to certain pests, diseases, or environmental conditions or produce a specific appearance or nutritional trait.

organisms. As new genes, and their associated traits, are discovered, they become available for use in genetic engineering. If a plant needs "antifreeze" to protect it from freezing, a scientist will look for a plant or animal with the antifreeze trait. Once the needed gene is snipped from the genetic code of the original organism, the next step is to insert the gene into the DNA of the new organism. Bacteria and viruses are used to carry genes inside the cells to which they are to be added. Scientists take advantage of the natural ability of bacteria and viruses to pass their genetic material through the cell walls of other organisms.

Certain soil bacteria called agrobacteria have long been recognized for their ability to invade plant cells and cause "tumors." You might even see one of these tumors if you watch for a tree branch with an ugly, unshapely knot. Scientists use agrobacteria as gene carriers for plants because of their known ability to invade plant cells. First, they use their "scissors" and "glue" to remove unwanted genes from agrobacteria and insert the new genes to be added to a plant. Next, the altered agrobacteria are mixed with bits of plant tissue. Some of the plant cells will be invaded by the bacteria. To be sure they get only the plant cells with agrobacteria, scientists also add an extra gene for a trait such as antibiotic resistance. When the plant cells are then grown in the presence of the antibiotic, only the cells with the added genes will survive. Finally, the bits of plant tissue modified with new genes will be used to make a whole plant. Several names are used to refer to organisms in which a gene has been inserted from another organism: "genetically modified," "genetically engineered," or "transgenic."

Developing a New Food Product

Demands for new plants or food products may come from growers, from social agencies concerned with malnutrition, or from food processors. Genetic engineers seek out a gene from any source that has the desired trait. For example, a silkworm gene has been used to protect grapevines from disease, and potatoes have been given a moth gene to protect from potato blight fungus. When using genetic engineering methods to transfer genes between organisms, it does not matter if the organisms are plant or animal. A gene snipped from a fish can as easily be added to a plant as a gene snipped from a daffodil.

Genetic engineering procedures require a well-equipped laboratory facility and highly trained personnel. Once a new organism is developed, a long testing process follows to see if the added gene results in the desired trait. After that, approval may be required from various government agencies to grow or sell the new plant. For example, scientists working to develop an improved variety of rice struggled for more than 10 years before they hit upon the necessary genetic changes. The new rice is still not in production because government approvals have not been obtained. Once approval is obtained, it still remains to be seen if consumers will accept the new product.

Improved Agricultural Production

The majority of genetically modified plants grown today have genes added that help with pest control. Better management of weed and insect pests leads to bigger crop yields. The cost of growing crops is reduced if the amount of herbicides and insecticides is reduced. Environmental benefits result if farmers do not have to plow their fields to kill weeds and if safer or fewer chemicals run off the fields into surrounding waterways.

The European corn borer is the corn farmer's nightmare. Major crop losses were common before insecticides were available to kill these hated insects. One insecticide was derived from a soil bacterium, *Bacillus thuringiensis*. These bacteria, usually referred to as Bt, produce a protein that is toxic to the digestive system of the corn borer. Even so, spraying crops with insecticides has never been totally successful; the spraying could miss some plants and leave them vulnerable, or weather conditions might interfere.

Finally, in the 1990s, genetic engineers developed a variety of corn into which they had transferred a Bt gene. Plants with this gene were able to produce the protein that was toxic to the corn borer. Since every cell of the new Bt corn contained the Bt gene, a corn borer that ate any part of the plant would get a toxic dose. A farmer who planted Bt corn no longer had to worry about corn borers.

Glyphosate is the most commonly used herbicide in the world. Home gardeners and industrial farmers alike rely on it to kill a wide assortment of weeds. To gardeners, an herbicide is only a matter of having a pretty garden. However, to farmers, it is a matter of whether crop yields are large enough to pay their bills and feed their families. Glyphosate kills plants by interfering with the

MONARCHS UNDER THREAT— OR ARE THEY?

Early in the days of growing Bt corn, an alarm was raised that the corn strain might be harmful to the beloved monarch butterfly. It was reasoned that pollen from the Bt corn would settle on the milkweeds that make up the monarch food supply. The monarchs would eat the toxic pollen along with the milkweed and die as a result. A university study that showed this to be the case received lots of publicity.

In an effort to resolve the controversy, the USDA organized a team of scientific experts to study whether monarch populations were being affected. Their studies found that Bt corn as grown in farm fields did not represent a threat to the monarchs. While there may still be many reasons for concern about the well-being of this beautiful butterfly, Bt corn is not regarded as a serious threat.

FIGURE 6.3 Genetically modified corn does not seem to be a hindrance to monarch butterflies.

production of a protein needed for growth. Genetic engineers figured out how to insert a gene in soybean plants that makes the plant cells resistant to the effects of glyphosate. Farmers who plant glyphosate-tolerant soybean seeds can kill the weeds in their field by spraying with glyphosate. The soybean crop is unaffected by the spray and will have a higher yield since plants are not competing with weeds.

Many other types of plants have been genetically engineered to improve crop yield. A genetically modified variety of papaya that resists a deadly virus has saved the Hawaiian papaya industry. Scientists are working to develop plants that can grow under stressful or changing environmental conditions. These efforts take on even greater importance in the face of changing climatic conditions. They may also help to feed growing populations in areas that are not well suited to agriculture.

Better Nutrition

What if broccoli tasted like chocolate? Would we all eat a lot of it and get healthier? Unfortunately, the appearance of chocolate-flavored broccoli at your grocery store is unlikely in the near future. This is because scientists are only beginning to understand the genetics of the cacao plant and how it yields the complex flavors in processed chocolate. Yet the production of fruits and vegetables with better natural flavor and appearance might encourage us to eat more of them.

In many Asian countries, rice is a staple food. Poor people in those countries may have little else to eat besides rice. Rice does not contain beta-carotene, an essential micronutrient for the production of vitamin A. Vitamin A deficiency can cause blindness and even death; in fact, it is a major public health problem in the developing world.

Genetic engineers had the idea to make rice that would provide the needed beta-carotene. They finally accomplished this by inserting both a bacteria gene and a corn gene into the DNA of rice. The new rice is called "golden rice" because the grains have a gold color. So far, this rice is not being grown anywhere despite the urgency of

Golden Rice

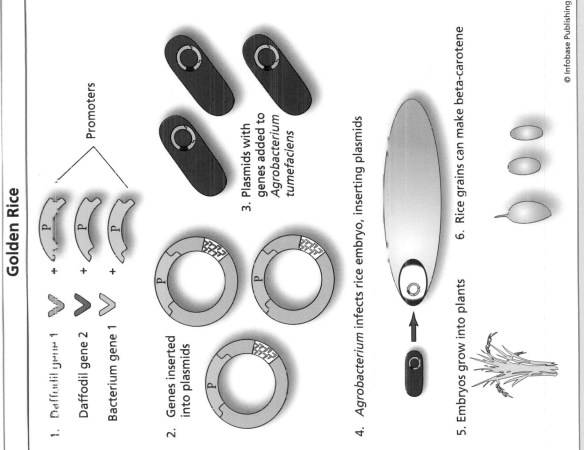

1. Daffodil gene 1
   Daffodil gene 2
   Bacterium gene 1

   Promoters

2. Genes inserted into plasmids

3. Plasmids with genes added to *Agrobacterium tumefaciens*

4. *Agrobacterium* infects rice embryo, inserting plasmids

5. Embryos grow into plants

6. Rice grains can make beta-carotene

FIGURE 6.4 To create golden rice, researchers isolated two genes from daffodils and one from a bacterium that, together, made possible the production of beta-carotene. They then added promoters (segments of DNA that turn genes on), which were inserted into circular combinations of genes in bacteria. Once the bacteria infected embryos (seeds) of rice plants, the beta-carotene genes were inserted. The seeds then grew into rice plants that produced grains that could make beta-carotene.

the problem it was created to address. For one thing, it is not clear if the beta-carotene will be effective in the diet unless it is accompanied by a source of fat. Without the fat, vitamin A cannot be used efficiently in the body. Some also fear that a small number of people will have an allergic reaction or some unexpected response to the new rice. Yet the bigger concern that has held up its use is the safety issue related to the introduction of genetically engineered crops into the environment. It is feared that the altered genes might escape and affect the standard rice crops or perhaps jump to a new species, leading to undesirable consequences.

ANIMALS AND GENETIC MODIFICATION

Genetic modification of livestock is technically difficult, but it is an area of active research. The fact that it takes animals long periods of time to reproduce and grow to maturity slows down the research process. Ranchers could raise genetically modified cattle that are disease resistant or that gain weight more quickly. Pharmaceutical companies are interested in developing dairy cattle that could produce medically useful proteins in their milk. One group is working to develop cattle that are incapable of getting mad cow disease. Furthest along in the development process is a salmon with a modified gene that speeds its growth. Fish producers plan to use the salmon in aquaculture, growing the fish in enclosed cages placed in coastal areas. The company is awaiting approval from the FDA. In the meantime, critics of the farmed fish have expressed fear that escaped fish will damage wild salmon populations by interbreeding with them.

ARE GENETICALLY MODIFIED FOODS SAFE TO EAT?

In the debates over "Frankenfoods" or how to save hungry people from starvation, assessing the safety of genetically modified foods is not an easy question to answer. Angry consumers and

GOLDEN RICE OR FOOL'S GOLD?

Ingo Potrykus and Peter Beyer are two very determined scientists. Dr. Potrykus, of the Golden Rice Humanitarian Board, based in Basel, Switzerland, and Dr. Beyer, of the University of Freiburg, Germany, met while they were on a trip to New York in the early 1990s to attend a meeting about rice, hosted by the Rockefeller Foundation. The Rockefeller Foundation wanted to address the problem of vitamin A deficiency in the developing world by devising a new variety of rice. According to the World Health Organization, from 250,000 to 500,000 children go blind each year due to vitamin A deficiency. Drs. Potrykus and Beyer took up the challenge and used their knowledge of **recombinant DNA technology** to modify the genetics of the rice plant. They succeeded in producing a rice variety that contains beta-carotene, which is converted to vitamin A in the human body. The beta-carotene gives the rice its yellow or golden color (the same beta-carotene that makes carrots orange). Their golden rice was the first genetically engineered food created specifically for a humanitarian purpose. After much delay to obtain approval for growing a genetically modified crop, an improved version was finally field-tested in Louisiana.

In 2006, Drs. Potrykus and Beyer were recognized by a group of fellow scientists as having made the most important contribution to agricultural biotechnology over the past decade. Despite this recognition, some food experts and humanitarian groups have questioned whether golden rice can achieve its intended purpose. Among their questions are whether the crop would grow well in areas where it is needed; if children would achieve adequate levels of vitamin A to prevent blindness; and if more children could be helped by using available resources for other projects, such as providing clean water. Some opponents object to golden rice as a public relations stunt created by the biotechnology industry that is aimed at convincing the public to accept genetically engineered foods.

attention-seeking media have proclaimed genetically modified foods to be dangerous, often with little scientific information to back up their positions. Thoughtful scientists have recommended careful testing of new products for safety before they are introduced to the public. There are large differences in attitudes toward genetically modified foods among different countries. For example, genetically modified crops are rare in European Union countries, largely because of consumer concerns over safety. On the other hand, the United States is the biggest producer of genetically modified crops, making up more than 50% of the worldwide crop acreage. Genetically modified crops became common in the United States during the 1990s with little public notice. The EPA approved the first Bt corn in 1995 after a nearly two-year review of scientific data. The new corn variety required EPA approval because it acted as a pesticide. Foods from plants engineered to contain a novel ingredient not commonly found in foods and those derived from genetically engineered animals undergo scientific review by the FDA prior to marketing. The FDA concluded that the foods derived from genetically modified plants contained proteins, fats, and carbohydrates that were essentially the same as those found in standard foods.

An area of particular concern with genetically modified foods is the possibility of the creation of unsuspected allergens in the proteins of introduced genes. For example, an attempt to transfer a gene from the Brazil nut into soybeans was abandoned because of the possibility of setting off allergies in people who are allergic to tree nuts. It is possible to test new foods for the presence of substances that are known allergens. But there is no way to test for new allergens that may result from the transfer of genes from bacteria or plants that have not previously served as food sources. In the future, it may be possible to screen for substances with certain chemical properties that make them more likely to react with the human immune system. Individuals with many allergies may need to identify and avoid foods from genetically modified sources.

Many foods that are produced from genetically engineered plants carry functioning antibiotic-resistant genes. These were introduced as extra genes during the gene-transfer process to aid in the selection of the modified plant cells. Some claim that these new genes might unexpectedly combine with intestinal bacteria, leading to the creation of antibiotic-resistant organisms. There is a small possibility that someone who is taking antibiotics could eat a food that contains a gene that would interfere with an antibiotic's effectiveness.

Perhaps the greatest concern regarding the safety of genetically modified foods is the possibility of unexpected consequences. For example, the new genes could react with other genes or take up contaminants from the soil to produce toxic substances in the body. Other problems might appear many years after genetically modified changes have been introduced into the food supply. While such events are regarded as unlikely, the consequences if they occur could be serious. There is no way to test for such unforeseen events, which is why some people are so cautious about the development of genetically modified food.

CLONING
The Hows and Whys of Cloning

Perhaps the milk carton on your breakfast table has a picture of the perfect milk cow. This healthy cow produces gallons of high-quality milk year after year. The dairy farmer breeds her in the hope that her female offspring will take on her many good traits. But the process of inheritance is uncertain. The offspring might take on the good traits of the mother cow, or they might instead take on traits inherited from the male cow (the bull). **Cloning** is a method of reproduction in which the "daughter" cows are guaranteed to be exact copies of their "mother" cow. They are essentially the mother's identical twin, but they are born at a different time.

Genetic scientists have only recently succeeded at the complex process of cloning mammals. In 1997, a sheep in Scotland became the most famous sheep of all time. She was the first mammal created by genetic cloning, and was given the name Dolly by the scientists who were responsible for her birth. Since then, scientists have succeeded in cloning various animals, including cattle. The process is expensive and inefficient. Most cloning attempts do not result in healthy offspring. Often, cloned animals develop health problems as they mature.

Cloned animals are created using a process called nuclear-transfer technology. The entire process involves two animals in addition to the one being cloned. First, an egg cell is obtained from the ovary of a female animal. The nucleus, which includes the genetic material of the first animal, is removed from the egg cell, leaving other parts of the cell intact. Next, a nucleus obtained from a cell of the animal to be cloned is transferred into the egg cell. This egg cell, which contains its new nucleus, is then stimulated with chemicals or electric current to cause it to divide. After a few cell divisions, an embryo results. All the cells in this embryo contain genetic material identical to that of the animal being cloned. The embryo is then placed into the uterus of yet another female animal, where it develops until birth.

Cloning technology is still too new and expensive to be used on a wide scale in the cattle industry. Still, it does provide a method for farmers and ranchers to preserve the genetic material of their best animals. They can reliably reproduce animals with the desired traits, such as a younger version of an aging but superior animal. Usually, these cloned animals would then produce offspring using conventional breeding methods. It is unlikely that the cloned animals would ever enter the food supply in any great quantity.

Safety of Cloned Foods

In 2008, the FDA announced their assessment that "meat and milk from clones of cattle, swine, and goats, and food from the sexually reproduced offspring of clones, are as safe to eat as food from conventionally bred animals." This followed years of study and data analysis by the agency. In the process, they consulted with teams of experts in the fields of food safety, toxicology, molecular biology, and animal studies. An extensive period for public comments was included, and all the issues raised were addressed by the FDA. FDA scientists concluded that it was not possible to distinguish a healthy cloned animal from a conventionally bred one. They further concluded that milk from cloned cows did not differ from milk from conventionally bred ones. The FDA did not require that meat or dairy products from cloned animals be labeled as such, since they were not distinguishable from other products. Most concerns about the cloning of livestock deal with the ethics and well-being of the animals, not the safety of food products.

REVIEW

Recent decades have seen rapid progress in the field of genetics, enabling the insertion of genes from the DNA of one organism into the DNA of another organism. Corn plants have been modified to include a gene that causes the plant to produce a chemical that is toxic to corn borers. A form of genetically modified soybean is resistant to the effects of a popular herbicide, allowing farmers to spray for weeds without harming the soybean crop. Research is ongoing to increase the nutritive value of plants through genetic modification. The FDA has tested genetically modified foods and concluded that their ingredients are essentially the same as those of conventional foods. Questions remain about the possible long-term effects of genetically modified crops on health and the environment. Animal cloning is another form of genetic modification that allows the production of livestock animals that are genetic replicas of a selected animal. The FDA has approved meat from cloned animals as being safe to eat, but practical considerations have limited the use of cloning.

7

DRINKING
WATER SAFETY

Sherlock Holmes might well know how to solve a case of arsenic poisoning—look for the characteristic symptoms, consider all the clues, and find the murderer. Nevertheless, the problem of arsenic has stumped the U.S. government, scientists, and regulators for years. Everyone agrees that arsenic is poison—that is not the issue. Even before Sherlock Holmes's day, arsenic was a favorite murder weapon. The problem for today's scientists is to figure out just how much arsenic can be in a water supply without killing someone, or otherwise harming their health. The amount should be as close to zero as possible—but how close is close enough? The arsenic standard is one of the thousands of issues faced every day by the people who are responsible for providing safe drinking water supplies.

WATER DISTRIBUTION

During the 1800s in America, the threats of typhoid and cholera were always present. Back then, people got their drinking water from nearby rivers or lakes, or from shallow wells. These water sources could easily be contaminated by sewage discharge. Once a bacterial disease like typhoid appeared in a community, it could be quickly spread through water sources that were contaminated with sewage runoff. At the turn of the twentieth century, city officials across the country were busy building systems to supply clean water. They built dams and water reservoirs to serve as storage systems, and complex networks of water mains and distribution pipes throughout the growing towns and cities to deliver water. Pumping stations and water towers provided the water pressure needed for indoor plumbing.

Clean drinking water also required a system for controlling wastewater. Initially, sewage was discharged into open ditches. The development of closed pipes (the so-called sanitary sewers) was a major improvement. Early collection systems provided no more than an organized way to get the sewage to a holding place until it was discharged to the nearest river. Once there, it would flow downstream where it would foul the next community's water supply. This short-sighted system gradually gave way to the modern sewage treatment facilities now present in all communities.

WATER TREATMENT AND SUPPLY

Drinking water comes either from surface sources, such as rivers and reservoirs, or from groundwater pumped from wells. Most public water supplies are treated before being sent through the distribution system. Solid particles are removed by settling and filtration. Disinfectants such as chlorine are added to kill any pathogens that might be present. Treatment methods vary somewhat depending on the natural chemicals and contaminants that may be in the local water source.

Unless we happen to live near a water treatment plant, it is possible to turn on the tap every morning without ever thinking about where our water comes from. The miles and miles of water and sewer pipes are for the most part invisible. But this invisibility leads to indifference, which could be a problem for the future of clean water. When a community takes its drinking water for granted, it is often unwilling to spend tax dollars to replace aging water mains or upgrade treatment plants. Engineering studies have revealed the existence of thousands of miles of pipes in U.S. cities that need replacement. Every leaky, old pipe is a possible source of contamination. Before lead pipes were banned, they were commonly used in water systems and in homes. The water supply in many older homes today has tap water containing lead at levels above the EPA limit.

REGULATION OF WATER SUPPLIES

Public water supply systems are regulated by the Safe Water Drinking Act of 1974. This act authorizes the EPA to set health-based standards for natural and man-made contaminants that might occur in drinking water. The original law specified 20 chemical contaminants. Since then, the number of regulated chemicals has been increased to 91. The EPA works with state agencies and local water suppliers to be sure the standards are met. Every local water supplier is required to provide an annual report to its customers. This report provides information about the source and quality of the water supply plus any contaminants that were detected.

For the most part, Americans enjoy very high-quality drinking water. Yet according to an analysis by the *New York Times*, 49 million Americans were provided with drinking water that did not meet EPA standards for bacteria or chemical concentrations in a five-year period beginning in 2004. Of even greater concern to water safety experts is that water supplies are tested for only 91 chemicals, while thousands of chemicals are used in U.S. industries. Many of these chemicals are known to cause cancer and other diseases at the low levels that might be found in drinking water. Recent studies suggest that even those few chemicals that are EPA-regulated may be at levels that make them a risk to human health.

FIGURE 7.1 Water is purified at the Hill Canyon Wastewater Treatment Plant in Camarillo, California.

Chemical contaminants in drinking water are of particular concern because we are constantly exposed to them. While the types of food we eat change constantly, everyone drinks water in some form every day. Diseases caused by low doses of a chemical contaminant would likely not occur for years. How do researchers figure out that consuming a certain chemical can increase one's risk of cancer or other disease? And if a chemical can cause cancer, how much of it can one consume without risking one's health? These are not easy questions to answer, which is why not all the experts agree on how much of a chemical contaminant is too much in a public water supply. Certainly, it is impossible to expose people to different doses of chemicals, and then wait years to see which of them get cancer. Instead, most of the information about chemicals and health risks comes from carefully controlled animal studies. Groups of mice or rats are given different doses of a chemical of interest. Then all the animals are carefully observed for any changes in their health. Based on results of these studies, researchers try to determine which level of a chemical is probably safe for humans.

An easy answer would be to say that no chemical should be allowed in our water supplies if it might cause disease. However,

CONTROLLING CONTAMINANTS IN CALIFORNIA

Residents of Los Angeles, California, can count themselves lucky that Dr. Pankaj Parekh is the one responsible for the quality of their drinking water. Dr. Parekh is serious about his responsibilities to the millions of people who drink Los Angeles water. When he learned that the city's

FIGURE 7.2 Dr. Pankaj Parekh, director of Water Quality for the City of Los Angeles Department of Water and Power, stands near the Ivanhoe Reservoir in Los Angeles. The reservoir is filled with black plastic balls to prevent sunlight from reaching contaminants in the water.

this would be an impossible goal. For one thing, many chemicals occur naturally in water supplies and are completely harmless at low levels. Most chemical contamination reaches water supplies from industrial or agricultural runoff. New industrial chemicals are developed every year, and every new industry means

water supply contained levels of bromate that might increase the risk of cancer, he wanted to take immediate action. His problem was that the bromate levels of the water met EPA standards as it was leaving the treatment plant. However, once the water reached the reservoir and spent time under the hot Los Angeles sun, the chemical reactions that took place resulted in higher bromate levels. Technically, the water supply was perfectly legal since the EPA requires only that the water be measured for bromate *at* the treatment plant. Still, Dr. Parekh knew that once the water was stored in the reservoir for awhile, it was not safe to drink. He and his colleagues came up with a clever solution— cover the reservoir with thousands of black floating balls! However, the complaints soon followed. Residents near the reservoir wanted it to look like a lake, not a bunch of black rubber balls. In the words of one resident, "They ruined the reservoir by putting black pimples all over it." Although Dr. Parekh explained the possible dangers of high bromate levels in the reservoir water supply, he had to admit that the water was perfectly legal according to EPA regulations.

The problem of Dr. Parekh and the black balls is but one example of why many experts think the 1974 Safe Water Drinking Act needs to be updated. In the decades since it was written, thousands of complex chemicals have been developed for industrial use. Scientists have learned much more about the risks of human exposure to many of these chemicals. On the other hand, the costs of controlling industrial pollution to keep it out of water supplies are prohibitive, according to industry spokesmen.

a new pollution source. The cost of removing every chemical from drinking water, or even testing for all of them, would be prohibitive.

RISKS TO WATER SUPPLIES
Industrial Waste

Discharge of industrial waste into waterways is regulated by the EPA, in cooperation with state water control agencies. Industries obtain permits that state the types and amounts of chemicals they can release. Much of this pollution comes from huge industries like chemical manufacturing and the plastics industry. However, some of it comes from small businesses such as the local dry cleaner. Many of the chemical pollutants end up in drinking water supplies.

Arsenic is only one of thousands of chemicals that are found in industrial waste. This waste product comes from many industries, including wood processing, steel, and mining. It can also occur naturally. Drinking water experts worry about it both because of its known health effects and because it is so widely present. Long-term exposure to arsenic at some levels can cause cancer. In 2006, following years of public discussion, the EPA lowered the allowable limit for arsenic in drinking water. Scientific debate continues about whether the new limit is low enough to protect public health. Industry groups emphasize the cost of cleaning up arsenic pollution, while health experts point to studies showing the chemical's risks to public health.

For years, coal-fired power plants have been spewing toxic pollutants into the air. Regulations intended to clean the air have helped to create a new source of industrial water waste. This liquid chemical waste comes from the scrubbers that are placed in power plant smokestacks to remove chemicals before they go into the air. Many of these chemicals end up being discharged into waterways, including dangerous chemicals like barium and arsenic. These new sources of water contamination present another problem for the people who are responsible for providing the public with clean drinking water.

Farm Runoff

Agricultural runoff is the biggest source of pollution affecting U.S. rivers and lakes. This pollution occurs as rain and snowmelt drain from farmland and carries with it bits of soil, chemicals, and organisms from animal waste. This type of pollution is called nonpoint source pollution since it comes from a wide area rather than from a point source such as an industrial pipe. The runoff products produced by modern farming methods can put drinking water supplies at risk.

In traditional farming, farmers often spread animal manure on their fields. In small amounts, this was a safe and efficient means to dispose of waste and to fertilize fields at the same time. However, today's animal feed lots produce enormous volumes of animal waste—more than can be safely disposed of. Excessive amounts of animal waste spread on fields are more than natural decomposition processes can handle. As a result, rainfall carries massive numbers of bacteria, viruses, and parasites from these wastes into rivers and groundwater.

Chemical fertilizers and pesticides applied to farm fields add to the pollution that leaves the farm through water runoff. Atrazine is one popular herbicide that is often used on corn fields. It is also one of the most common contaminants found in U.S. drinking water. Recent research shows that, even at EPA-approved levels, atrazine may cause birth defects and reproductive problems in humans. Scientists point out that even very small doses of chemicals can have critical effects at certain growth stages, such as during development of the fetal brain.

Atrazine levels in drinking water go up and down throughout the year. The highest levels tend to occur in spring at about the time farm fields are being sprayed. However, a public water supply may be tested for atrazine as seldom as once a year. The

(continues on page 124)

MYSTERY IN MILWAUKEE

One spring weekend in Milwaukee, Wisconsin, a local TV station carried an odd news story—drugstores all around town were selling out of anti-diarrhea medicines. The following day, doctors' offices were fielding hundreds of calls from patients who were sick with an intestinal illness. Meanwhile, schools scrambled to find substitutes for the teachers who called in sick. Yet when school bells actually rang, the low number of available teachers was not a problem because so few students showed up. The urgent situation quickly came to the attention of city health officials. They recognized they had a problem, but did not know what it was. Their first step was to get answers to the four Ws of outbreak investigations: (1) Who is getting sick? (2) What is the disease? (3) Where do the sick people live, work, and go to school? And (4) when did they get sick?

Those who were stricken reported symptoms that could have been caused by any of dozens of pathogens. Initial laboratory tests failed to turn up any infectious organisms. A call to the state health department convinced officials that the outbreak was limited to the city of Milwaukee. The head of the city's water treatment department assured officials that the city's water had passed all tests for quality. Milwaukee gets its drinking water from Lake Michigan, and the only unusual recent finding was excessive cloudiness in the water.

Several frantic days passed as hospitals dealt with the large numbers of sick people, laboratory workers continued to test patient specimens, and the public anxiously waited for news of what was happening while they feared for their health. Suspicion was slow to fall on the water supply because regular testing found no problems. Finally, a laboratory technician at a local hospital noticed something on a specimen slide she had never seen before. She decided to prepare another slide by using a special technique and found that the sample was teeming with a para-site called *Cryptosporidium*.

Cryptospiridium are parasites that live inside a hard protective shell called an *oocyst*. Once they are inside human intestines, the parasites lose their shell and infect the intestinal walls. Infection by this parasite explained the patients' symptoms. This parasite occurs naturally in surface water supplies in low numbers and is normally removed during water filtration. Could it have been in the Milwaukee water supply in great enough numbers to make so many people sick?

The mystery could only be solved by testing a large volume of water—enough to run through a filter and come up with the few-and-far-between parasites. Yet that day's water would not do. The laboratory needed water samples from almost two weeks earlier, before most of the people fell ill. Some old samples were available, but they did not provide nearly enough volume. Finally, someone remembered that ice suppliers constantly pulled water from the city supply and froze it into huge chunks. Sure enough, the local ice plant had just what they needed: ice made from water taken from the city supply weeks earlier. Frozen deep inside the ice blocks were the answers to the mystery. Once they melted the ice samples, they found thousands of *Cryptospiridium* oocysts. Although the original source of the *Cryptospiridium* contamination was never known, spring rains or snowmelt likely washed it from agricultural areas into Lake Michigan, the source of Milwaukee's drinking water. The cloudy water noted by the water department was further evidence for this explanation.

By the time the 1993 outbreak was over, more than 400,000 people had become sick, and close to 100 had died. Since then, Milwaukee has spent millions of dollars to extend their intake pipe farther into Lake Michigan to assure a cleaner water source. They and many other water systems now add ozone during water treatment in order to kill *Cryptospiridium*. The outbreak served as a wake-up call to water supply managers across the country. They must do more than meet the required tests to be sure their water supplies are safe.

(continued from page 121)

water is legal as long as the average amount of the chemical does not exceed EPA regulations. High atrazine levels might not be detected during their spring peaks, or might be "averaged away" by lower levels during the rest of the year. Once atrazine is in the water source for a public water supply, it is costly to remove. In 2009, 43 water systems in agricultural states joined a lawsuit against the manufacturer of atrazine, seeking to force the manufacturer to pay for removing the chemical from drinking water.

Following continued public concern about atrazine in drinking water, EPA officials have agreed to conduct a scientific review of the chemical and its possible health effects. But research funding for the EPA is in short supply, and without additional study, atrazine may turn out to be another hazardous chemical that escapes EPA review. Even if new findings suggest that atrazine should be strictly regulated, it is not certain this will happen. Sometimes, regulations are weakened, or proposed laws are stopped by powerful congress-people who represent farming states. Because atrazine is such a cheap and effective herbicide, farmers emphasize to their congress-people how important it is for maintaining high corn crop yields.

Bioterrorism

Water supplies are a natural target for terrorists and other criminals because water is so essential to human life. However, certain features of our water supplies do offer some protection. For instance, any chemical or pathogen added to a large water reservoir would be so diluted by the time it reached individuals that it is unlikely to be a risk to human health. Water supplies are also protected by disinfection methods that are used during water treatment. Most supplies are treated with chlorine, which remains in the water as it flows through the distribution system. Chlorine kills most pathogens that might be introduced after water leaves the treatment plant. However, chlorine offers no protection from toxic chemicals. The U.S. Department of Homeland Security, along with the EPA, works with local water systems to assure adequate protection of water supplies.

TAP VS. BOTTLED WATER

Many people choose to purchase bottled water, perhaps because they think it is healthier than tap water. This is not necessarily the case. Bottled water, which is regulated by the FDA, is not required to undergo as much testing as the water that comes from public water systems. In fact, much bottled water *is* tap water. Consumers who buy bottled water should check the labels and know what they are buying and think about why they are buying it. Some persons with special needs (such as those with severely compromised immune systems) may need to protect themselves from possible tap water contamination by locating a reliable source of high-quality bottled water to drink.

REVIEW

In pre-twentieth-century America, threats of illness from drinking water came mostly in the form of bacteria that were spread by sewage contamination of the water supply. Outbreaks of diseases such as cholera and typhoid were quite common and greatly feared. The advent of modern water treatment methods and sanitary sewage systems has eliminated these threats in the United States, but new threats have replaced them. Chemicals from industrial processes and agricultural runoff find their way into public water supplies and prove difficult to remove. Health-based standards for chemicals allowable in drinking water are determined by the EPA. Toxic chemicals such as arsenic and atrazine are frequently detected in tests of public water supplies. Some scientists are concerned that the levels at which these chemicals occur, and the fact that so many people are exposed to them over long periods of time, may impact public health. Suspected health effects, such as reproductive problems and cancer, may appear only after many years of exposure, making it difficult to assess the impact of chemical pollutants in drinking water.

8

INTENTIONAL CONTAMINATION OF THE FOOD SUPPLY

"**Y**ou prefer white bread? Yes, I can make white bread for you," a nineteenth-century English baker might have said to a working-class customer. Back then, it was the fashion among the rich to eat the whitest of bread; even poor people wanted to appear rich by eating white bread. Yet white bread could only be produced from high-quality flours, making the bread too expensive for most budgets. Still, a baker was in the business of selling bread, and the way to sell more bread was to give the English housewife or servant what she or he wanted. This dilemma led to the widespread custom of adding alum, a bleaching agent, to bread that was made with low-quality flour. Everyone was happy: The baker sold his bread, the housewife or servant had bread as white as the rich folks, and because the alum was not really poisonous, nobody grew sick or died.

Food tampering has been with us for as long as food has been bought and sold, as farmers, processors, and sellers have sought ways to sell more food and increase their profits. Some of the earliest cases of food tampering were harmless to health. It was only a matter of cheating the customers by not providing them with the quality of food they expected. But other cases were more serious, even to the extreme that food was contaminated with poisonous substances. The simple transaction of buying and selling food has always required a significant amount of trust on the part of the food consumer. Sometimes, that trust has been violated.

With the twenty-first century come new worries about the intentional contamination of food supplies. Modern technologies have provided the means to cause widespread illness simply by the introduction of poisons or pathogens into food sources. Anyone with access to a bit of scientific expertise and a job in food production could contaminate the food supply of thousands of people. Terrorists who wish to cause death, disrupt a country's economy, or spread fear within it know that **bioterrorism** is an effective means of accomplishing these goals. Just as countries raise armies to provide for defense, it is essential that government agencies be on guard against threats to a nation's food supply.

ADULTERATING FOOD FOR PROFIT

As discussed, accidental food contamination initially came about as a result of how food is grown or processed. Although such contamination may result from carelessness or attempts at cost-cutting, it is not really intentional. The term *adulteration* is generally used for cases in which food is intentionally tampered with. For instance, processors may try to make a food product seem more valuable or more wholesome than it really is by diluting it or substituting one of its ingredients with a cheaper substance. American consumers are protected from food adulteration by laws that prohibit the addition of additives or food substitutes other than those stated on the label. Most food producers are too concerned about the reputations of their food brands to risk selling adulterated foods.

Laboratory testing by government agencies confirms the quality of our foods. Unfortunately, food swindlers keep coming up with new ways to fool the tests. Scientists who work as food "detectives" struggle to keep one step ahead as these swindlers concoct new ways to produce counterfeit food.

Take, for example, the case of the suspicious basmati rice. While cooks are willing to pay a higher price for this fine, flavorful rice, they want to be sure they are getting the real thing. In response to reports of suspicious rice, food inspectors went to work to devise new genetic methods to test the rice. After sophisticated genetic analysis of rice samples, inspectors learned that many products that were labeled "basmati" were actually mixed with inferior types of rice. Methods like those used for DNA fingerprinting of crime suspects showed that the DNA of the inferior rice did not match the DNA of real basmati rice.

Food safety regulations are less strict in some foreign countries. We live in a global economy, where food imports flow into the United States through hundreds of ports of entry. The FDA and USDA are responsible for assuring that these imports meet U.S. food safety standards. However, the sheer volume of imports means that only a tiny portion of them can undergo thorough inspection. Also, among the thousands of possible chemicals that might be added to foods, only certain kinds of them are tested for safety.

In 2008, after a scandal in China involving the adulteration of milk with melamine, the FDA increased its testing for that substance. Melamine is a nitrogen-rich organic chemical used in making plastics and countertops. Melamine is known to cause serious kidney damage, and using it as a food additive is banned by national and international laws. Some Chinese milk producers were already adding water to raw milk so they could make a bigger profit on milk sales. The addition of melamine to watered-down milk enabled the milk to appear to have the proper level of nitrogen when it was inspected before being allowed into the marketplace. Unfortunately, many Chinese children died, and thousands were made sick before the practice was stopped. Rigorous

FIGURE 8.1 Chinese workers collect tainted milk powder for destruction or burying in Shangrao, China, on November 19, 2008. The Chinese government launched a major campaign to recover tainted milk powder and reform its dairy industry in the wake of melamine contamination found in infant formula.

FDA inspections found melamine to be present in a few processed foods imported from China. All of these products were recalled.

Consumer demands for cheap food continue to put pressure on food manufacturers to cut corners to produce cheaper products. Researchers who study food safety warn that current inspection systems are not adequate to compensate for these pressures, especially in regard to imported foods.

FOOD TAMPERING

Have you ever been annoyed by a safety seal on a food package that seems impossible to remove? These safety seals first appeared in the 1980s following several incidents of tampering with food or drug products on store shelves. In one case, several people died as a result of poisoned Tylenol pills. These acts were mostly committed by deranged individuals whose motives remain unknown.

As a result of these scandals, the U.S. Congress passed the Federal Anti-tampering Act, making it illegal to tamper with packaged food or drugs, while food manufacturers responded by devising special packaging so that the buyer could detect product tampering. Today, food jars have pop-up devices or plastic ring seals, dairy packaging comes with safety seals, and bagged

TOO SICK TO VOTE?

The followers of self-styled guru Bhagwan Shree Rajneesh were all set to build their world headquarters in a small Oregon community in 1984. The completion of their plans hinged on a county election that would allow construction to go forward. But suddenly a kink was thrown in their plans when an election law decision made it unlikely that their candidates could prevail. In response, fanatical cult members hatched a plan to contaminate the local water supply with vials of *Salmonella typhimurium*. They hoped that unsuspecting residents who drank the water would get a bad case of diarrhea and stay home on Election Day. The schemers did a test run by hiding vials of bacteria in the sleeves of their robes and sprinkling it on salad bars at local restaurants. As a result, the food from these contaminated salad bars made 751 people sick, and several were hospitalized. However, the final plan to contaminate the water system was never carried out.

State and CDC investigators were slow to discover the intentional nature of the outbreak. There was little news coverage at first, and careless restaurant workers were thought to be the source. More than a year later, suspicion turned to the cult, and several members were charged and imprisoned. A search of their commune turned up a copy of *The Anarchist Cookbook*, a book about explosives and bioterrorism.

products are difficult to tear open. Fortunately, these measures have been successful and food tampering is no longer a serious concern.

BIOTERRORISM AND THE FOOD SUPPLY
Is Our Food Supply at Risk?

When terrorism is a threat, the food supply presents a possible route of attack. Centralized food-processing systems and global trade in food present many opportunities for those who seek to harm others. Food pathogens may be particularly attractive to terrorists because they are available, inexpensive, and require little special knowledge. A small amount of contaminant could be easily concealed and smuggled into a central food- or water-processing facility. From there, the food-distribution system could spread contaminated food quickly to thousands of people. The tremendous growth of the biotechnology industry means that more people have access to modern scientific methods. Terrorists could use these methods to genetically alter bacteria to make them more dangerous, or to produce new toxins.

A special commission appointed by the U.S. Congress warned in 2008 that "the biological threat is greater than the nuclear." It would be easier for terrorists to acquire and use deadly pathogens than it would be for them to gain access to weapons-grade uranium or plutonium. The report concluded with a recommendation that prevention of biological terrorism be made a higher priority of the U.S. government.

Protecting the Food Supply

Public health officials have been concerned about protecting the food supply for decades. At first, heavy reliance was placed on spot-checks in food production facilities and on random sampling of foods at the point of sale. These more threatening times call for emphasis on preventing food attacks close to their source. Such attacks could come anywhere along the complex food supply chain. The first concern relates to control of pathogens or harmful chemicals that could be added to food or water supplies. Secondly, crop or livestock production could be disrupted on a large scale. The introduction of genetically altered organisms might cause a fast-spreading disease among poultry or cattle. "Superweeds," or plants that are resistant to common pesticides, could bring about crop failures. Lastly, terrorists could interfere with the means of transportation. Urban residents depend on continuous deliveries of foods to their grocery stores and restaurants. If fresh food supplies failed to arrive for even a few days, large-scale panic could result.

FDA GOES ONLINE TO PROTECT OUR FOOD

CARVER+Shock is the name of a sophisticated online "weapon" that serves on the front lines of the U.S. food defense system. It was originally developed by the U.S. military to identify areas that might be open to enemy attack. It is now available to food processors to help them identify spots in their manufacturing process that might provide an opening for food terrorists. The FDA and the USDA adapted and computerized the tool for use regarding food and agriculture safety issues. Formerly, agency officials would visit food-processing plants and ask employees a series of questions. This process might involve 20 or 30 people and take two to three days. With CARVER+Shock, the process can be accomplished by a small group of experts at the plant in less than a day.

The tool first requires a flow diagram of the food process to be analyzed. It then asks a series of questions about each step in the process. The program then assigns a score to each step based on how easy it would be to attack the process at that point and how much damage could be done. The idea is to help food industry managers to think like an attacker. Once weak points are identified, the company can take appropriate measures to reduce the risk of food contamination.

After the terrorist attacks of September 11, 2001, new government programs have been introduced to deal specifically with threats to the food supply. The food supply chain has been analyzed to find its weakest points. By learning where it would be easiest for terrorists to attack, officials and businesspeople alike can take countermeasures to head off attacks. More efforts have been assigned to vulnerable points. There is more cooperation among federal and local governments, as well as with academic researchers, to address the issue of bioterrorism. Educational materials have been developed for management and workers in the food industry to make them more aware of possible threats. International agencies work worldwide to provide an early warning system of attacks.

However, according to some food supply experts, the emphasis on terrorist threats has diverted attention from more likely health risks. These experts claim that an overall focus on more nutritional food, protected from all contamination, either accidental or intentional, could have more impact on public health. In addition, improved communications among countries and aid to those living in poverty could reduce international threats.

Mechanisms are in place to protect our food supply right now. However, it is impossible to be sure if they are adequate, or if bioterrorism threats are overblown.

REVIEW

Federal law prohibits the substitution of ingredients or inclusion of food additives that are not listed on the labels of processed foods. Although most food manufacturers closely adhere to regulations, consumer demand for cheap food occasionally results in reports of food substitutions or adulteration. The problem is particularly acute for foods that are imported from other countries where food regulations are less strict. Government inspectors are able to test only a small portion of imported foods for possible adulteration. The past decade has raised new alarms about the possibility of intentional food contamination by terrorists who wish to accomplish their social or political goals by harming others. Large-scale food-manufacturing and distribution systems provide the means for a contaminant such as a pathogen to be introduced and quickly distributed to grocery stores and restaurants over a wide area. New procedures are being implemented by food processors and government agencies to ensure that food and water supplies are protected from terrorists.

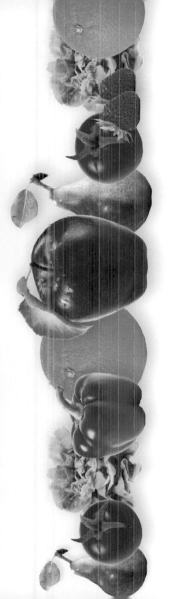

9

FUTURE OF FOOD SAFETY

If our food is making so many of us sick, why are we not doing something about it? Part of the answer is that most of us do not get very sick even if we happen to eat contaminated food. Typically, after a day or two of intestinal symptoms, we feel better and would rather forget about it. We often do not know which of the dozens of food items we ate was to blame, or if it was a food that made us ill in the first place. Yet as outbreaks of serious illness associated with foods continue to occur, many scientists, elected officials, and alarmed consumers think it is time to take actions to improve food safety. In the words of food safety advocate and U.S. Senator Tom Harkin (D Iowa), "On the whole, Americans enjoy safe and wholesome food. But, let's be honest, our food can be safer and it must be safer."

DECIDING WHAT WE MEAN BY FOOD SAFETY

How does one go about deciding if a particular food is safe? This is often not a simple question. For example, as popular as peanut butter sandwiches are, they are not safe to eat for someone with a peanut allergy. Unpasteurized cheese may not be safe for a pregnant woman. And what about lettuce that becomes contaminated with just a touch of arsenic? What about those people who are convinced that eating artificially manipulated genes will make them sick—do they regard genetically modified corn as being safe?

To a scientist, determining if a particular food is safe to eat is a matter of conducting careful scientific experiments. These may involve laboratory tests, animal studies, or epidemiology studies of selected populations. For example, an experiment to evaluate pesticide safety might use several groups of mice, with each group receiving a different dose of the pesticide in its feed. Perhaps the researchers observe no health effects in those animals that were fed low doses, and so they reason that small amounts of the pesticide will not threaten public health. As these conclusions are made available to other scientists and the general public, there may be disagreements about the results of the research and about what is an acceptable risk to public health.

At this point, decisions about food safety leave the realm of science and enter the realm of social values. How much risk does someone want to accept when eating peaches for breakfast or raw oysters in August? Politics becomes involved when decisions have broader consequences for financial interests, such as farm families concerned about keeping their farms or large industries concerned about their profit margins. Some decisions about food safety are made in the court of public opinion. Many people consider not only the health risks but also their personal beliefs and values when they decide what foods they will eat. Studies show that people are less willing to accept food risks that may arise from unfamiliar technology, or if experts disagree about the levels of risks. They also want risks to be

WEIGHING A BAN ON RAW OYSTERS

Raw oysters are an extremely popular dish. And some people who love them are willing to eat them year-round, even in the summer months when the chance of bacterial contamination is high. Oysters are harvested along the U.S. Gulf Coast where the waters are likely to be contaminated with *Vibrio* bacteria during the warmest months of the year. Persons with certain chronic health conditions are especially vulnerable to *Vibrio* infection if they eat contaminated oysters. Each year, many people become seriously ill after eating raw oysters. Some of them experience kidney failure, loss of limbs, and even death, despite education campaigns that attempt to warn about the dangers of eating raw oysters in warm months.

In 2009, the FDA proposed a ban on the sale of raw Gulf Coast oysters during warm months, unless the oysters had undergone a process *(continues)*

FIGURE 9.1 Raw oysters can be contaminated year-round, but especially in the summer, when warm weather encourages bacterial growth.

(continued)

to kill bacteria. In the words of an FDA official, "Seldom is the evidence on a food safety problem and solution so unambiguous." Yet despite the evidence, the FDA proposal provoked a huge outcry from Gulf Coast congresspeople and the oyster industry. The FDA was forced to delay the proposed regulation.

In the opinion of the Center for Science in the Public Interest, this was an example of public health losing out to the forces of special interests, in this case, the oyster industry. In response, others noted the small number of *Vibrio* infections in comparison to some other foodborne illnesses and suggested the FDA should target their limited resources on other food safety areas.

voluntary and prefer some sense of control over them. Since it is almost never possible to prove that a food is perfectly safe, public acceptance depends on how well their values are taken into consideration. Government officials who make decisions about food safety must do so based on the best available scientific information. They must also be aware of public opinion and social values related to food.

IMPROVING FOOD PRODUCTION AND PROCESSING METHODS

Irradiation

Irradiation is a method of processing food to destroy bacteria, parasites, or insects. The technology is similar to procedures that have long been used in medical and dental offices. Irradiation does not make food radioactive, as some people fear. It may cause very small changes in taste or nutritional value and adds to the cost of food processing. The safety of irradiated foods has been extensively tested in animal studies, with no evidence of health effects. A few foods are not suitable for irradiation; for example, irradiation of eggs in shells causes the egg whites to become milky.

Irradiation has proved effective at reducing or eliminating organisms from fruits, vegetables, meat, poultry, and spices. The FDA and USDA have approved its use on most foods. It would not substitute for other bacteria-reduction measures in the produce and meatpacking industry. Rather, it would provide an extra margin of protection against harmful bacteria. Nevertheless, irradiation is seldom used, largely due to consumer resistance. Studies have shown that consumers are more likely to purchase irradiated foods if they understand how irradiation makes food safer to eat. Foods that have been irradiated must be labeled with a distinctive logo called a "radura."

FIGURE 9.2 Irradiated foods carry this symbol on packaging or stickers on the product.

Livestock Animal Vaccination

Food safety begins where food originates: on farms and ranches. Food processing methods, government inspections, and consumer precautions cannot make up for all the sources of contamination that might arise on the farm. We depend on farmers to eliminate food risks as much as possible by careful pesticide use, use of sanitary procedures to keep their animals healthy, control of animal waste, and other measures.

Researchers are looking for ways to help farmers improve food safety. Their work has led to a new vaccine that can protect cattle from *E. coli* O157:H7. Cattle don't get sick from this form of *E. coli*, and many may have it in their systems without farmers knowing it. However, the more cattle shipped to slaughterhouses with *E. coli* O157:H7, the more likely it is that some of the bacteria will end up contaminating the meat supply. Recent outbreaks of serious illness from *E. coli* O157:H7 infection in humans have caused researchers and government officials to make the cattle vaccine a high priority. While it has the potential to greatly reduce the risk of *E. coli* O157:H7 illness in humans, the costs involved would be considerable. Farmers do not have the incentive to spend the money to vaccinate their animals since the cattle appear otherwise to be perfectly healthy. The question is: Would consumers be willing to pay more for their hamburgers if they knew the meat would be more likely to be free of *E. coli* O157:H7 contamination?

Genetics

Much of the future progress in food safety will not come from farms or food-processing plants, but from laboratories where geneticists are studying the DNA of food crops. The safety of genetically modified foods is likely to remain controversial for some time. Scientific experiments can answer concerns about whether genetically modified foods lead to risk of allergies, or whether genetically modified crops cause environmental hazards. But even without using genetic modification, there is much that genetic knowledge can contribute to the task of keeping our food safe. Genetic methods are helping to identify and eliminate pathogens during food processing and storage. By studying the genetics of the O157:H7 variant of *E. coli*, scientists are learning why it poses such a risk to public health and how to combat it. The need for pesticides may be reduced as plant scientists learn more about the genetics of plants' natural resistance to pests.

A system called PulseNet is using genetic methods to track down sources of foodborne illness outbreaks. The system uses a method of DNA fingerprinting to match samples of bacteria that are suspected of causing an outbreak. Samples taken from sick persons are analyzed in designated laboratories around the country. The DNA fingerprints of the suspected bacteria are then electronically transmitted to a national database at the CDC center in Georgia. If the DNA fingerprints from several samples match up, scientists are alerted to the presence of a foodborne illness outbreak. Bacteria from suspected food sources also undergo DNA fingerprinting. If the fingerprints match those taken from sick people, this may pinpoint the food source. The electronic system allows quick matching, even if cases are widely scattered across the country. In the future, more laboratories will be added to the system, and improved fingerprinting methods and communication will speed up the identification of outbreaks.

Geneticists are analyzing the genetic makeup of several fruits and vegetables with the intent to use this information to produce better crops. Once a gene with desirable properties is identified, plants that carry this gene can be bred selectively using conventional methods. For example, plant scientists could select a cantaloupe with genes for disease resistance or a grain that naturally produces more beta-carotene. Since fruits and vegetables are produced by conventional methods, the produce would not meet with the resistance that some consumers feel toward genetically modified crops.

IMPROVING GOVERNMENT OVERSIGHT

If you get sick after eating a chicken salad sandwich and a cup of soup, which government agency would you hold responsible for not preventing the problem: the agency that inspects poultry products, one of the four agencies that oversees eggs, or maybe the agency that controls pesticides applied to lettuce crops? It may even make a difference if your soup contained beef or chicken broth, or if your sandwich had one slice of bread or two. The system of food safety regulation in the United States is a patchwork of authority that is "outdated, underfunded, and overwhelmed," according to one elected official. Ever since the public outcry that greeted Upton Sinclair's exposé of filthy slaughterhouses in 1906, Congress has reacted to food scares with legislation that met the problems of the times. Budgets were increased to hire more food inspectors, but never at a pace fast enough to keep up with rapidly expanding food industries.

The FDA, which is responsible for the majority of food regulations, must devote many resources to its other (some would say main) role of overseeing drug safety. The Department of Agriculture is responsible for regulating food, along with assisting farmers and promoting agricultural products. These three roles sometimes come into conflict. While most government officials and food safety experts agree that improved food safety is of primary importance, there is little agreement on how best to make it happen.

One repeated suggestion for improving food safety is the creation of a single food agency. This could close gaps in the current system and eliminate wasteful duplication among agencies. Yet it would also threaten a powerful government bureaucracy and relationships that have been built up with the food industry and with Congress. As an intermediate step toward change during his first year in office, President Barack Obama created the position of FDA Deputy Commissioner of Foods. The commissioner's office is responsible for unifying all food safety activities within the FDA and will serve as a central contact with other government agencies. Pending legislation may give the agency expanded author-

NASA GIVES A BOOST TO FOOD SAFETY

Participants in the early days of the space program had a lot on their minds, including the challenges involved in sending people to the moon and getting them safely back to Earth. Yet in the midst of all that, someone had to think long and hard about what the astronauts would eat on the way there and back. No one even knew if it would be possible for astronauts to eat or digest food in the weightlessness of space. The first astronauts ate bland food sauces squeezed from a tube. Making sure the food was safe was more important than what it tasted like. The last thing an astronaut circling Earth or flying to the moon needed to worry about was a case of food poisoning.

The National Aeronautic and Space Administration (NASA), which oversees the U.S. space program, called on the Pillsbury Company to help them prepare meals for the astronauts. As a way of assuring the safety of the foods they prepared, NASA asked Pillsbury to use the same system their own engineers used to design spacecrafts. This system identified critical control points, or CCPs, where things might go wrong. In the food-manufacturing process, these were the points at which pathogens might enter the system. The goal was to measure and control conditions at every critical point in order to eliminate pathogens. Measurements were recorded so inspectors could review all steps of the process at any time. The system that Pillsbury developed was given the name **HACCP** (pronounced *has-sip*), for *Hazard Analysis Critical Control Point*.

The program was quite revolutionary in the food industry at the time. Until then, it seems no one had ever thought to do anything more than check the final food product for pathogens. If the inspectors found a problem, how could they trace it back to where it originated and fix it? Food manufacturing had by then developed into complex processes with lots of opportunities for contamination. HACCP gave food inspectors and the food industry a whole new way to tackle the problem. It put the emphasis on eliminating hazards and preventing contamination.

(continues)

(continued)

It also placed the burden of food safety on the producers rather than the government inspectors who came around only at the end of the process. Pillsbury recognized the value of the new system for commercial food production and immediately began to apply it for some of their own products.

Food scientists saw HACCP as a science-based approach that would improve food safety. But many in the food industry objected to it as an expensive and unwanted change to the way they had always done things. Controversy over this new approach to food safety continued for years in the U.S. Congress and in the media. Then came the Jack in the Box scandal, the first major outbreak of *E. coli* O157:H7 hamburger contamination. After that, arguments swayed to the side of requiring HACCP procedures in the meat and poultry industries. In the future, all processed food may be manufactured under the system first developed in the space program.

ity to recall suspect foods and increased funding for inspecting domestic and imported foods.

CONSUMER ACTION FOR FOOD SAFETY

Without thinking about it, consumers make choices relating to food safety at every meal, such as: Is that leftover meatloaf safe to eat? Did that peach come from a local grower or a foreign country? Does this restaurant appear to put high priority on hygiene? Did Mom check the label on the new cereal to be sure it will not affect my allergies? Is this hamburger thoroughly cooked? But for the informed consumer who is concerned about food safety, there are plenty of additional opportunities to play an active role in reducing public health risks that are associated with food.

Food Selection and Handling

Government agencies, food producers, grocers, and restaurants all work hard to provide the public with a safe food supply. But even with all safety measures in place, microorganisms or chemicals may sometimes be present at levels that pose a health risk. Since it is not possible to detect contaminants by sight, smell, or taste, it is essential to practice good sanitation at all times and to follow the rules for safe food handling and preparation. This is particularly important for members of groups at high risk of foodborne illness, such as those with compromised immune systems. A wealth of food safety information is available at a government Web site, www.foodsafety.gov, including an opportunity to ask questions of an expert. Some general guidelines for safe eating follow:

- Think about food safety when choosing foods and beverages. Know which foods have a higher risk of being contaminated. Read labels carefully, especially if you have a food allergy. Pay attention to dates on products.

- Because bacteria grow quickly at temperatures between 40°F (4.4°C) and 140°F (60°C), perishable food must be kept cold and eaten in a timely manner. Ground beef, for example, should be eaten or frozen within two days of purchase. Purchase perishable foods last when shopping, and get them home to the refrigerator or freezer as quickly as possible. Do not leave prepared foods out of the refrigerator for more than two hours. Finally, when storing leftovers, use shallow containers that allow foods to chill quickly.

- Wash your hands thoroughly before eating or preparing food. Avoid food preparation if you are sick. Wash raw produce before eating. Sanitize kitchen surfaces with a disinfectant, such as a chlorine solution.

- Avoid cross-contamination. Never allow raw meats to come in contact with foods that are already cooked or that will be eaten raw. Use hot, soapy water to wash hands and surfaces that come in contact with raw meats.

Use separate cutting boards and utensils for meat and nonmeat items.

● Cook all foods to the recommended temperatures, and use a food thermometer to check the internal temperature. Ground beef should be cooked to an internal temperature of 160°F (71°C), while poultry should reach an internal temperature of 165°F (74°C). Cooking temperatures for all foods are available on the government Web site.

● Only drink water from an approved water supply and avoid unpasteurized milk or fruit juices.

● To report a suspected case of foodborne illness, contact your local health department.

Choosing to Buy Organic

Many consumers choose to buy organic foods for nutritional reasons or to benefit the environment and often both. One additional benefit of purchasing organic foods is a reduced risk of the presence of pesticides and other ingredients that may give rise to health concerns. Foods labeled as "USDA Certified Organic" come from farms that have been inspected and certified as following the rules for organic production. According to these rules, fruits and vegetables have not been treated with synthetic pesticides or fertilized with synthetic chemicals or sewage sludge. They have not been genetically modified

FIGURE 9.3 The USDA allows for the placement of these labels on products that come from farms that inspectors have inspected and identified as being organic.

GOOD INFORMATION WHILE YOU SHOP

A California company called GoodGuide has compiled data and assigned ratings to thousands of food products. Sources for data include government databases, studies from universities and nonprofit organizations, and their own research. A user can either enter a product name or use a mobile phone camera to scan an item's bar code. In addition to an overall ranking for a product, the service provides information such as whether a food contains an ingredient known to cause cancer. It also provides information about the environmental impact of a product.

or irradiated. Organic meats must come from animals that have been fed with organic feed and must not have been treated with hormones or antibiotics.

Organic foods are almost always more costly than their nonorganic counterparts. Organic farming is usually done on a smaller scale and requires more labor-intensive methods. Organic feed for livestock is more expensive than nonorganic feed. The organic certification process adds a small additional cost. Despite the higher costs, the consumer demand for organic products continues to expand. Many consumers may choose either conventional or organic, depending on reported pesticide levels in the conventional product. Mobile phone applications (apps) can even provide this information on the spot. Most grocery stores now carry a large selection of organic foods. As more consumers choose to eat organic, and as more farmers use organic methods on a larger scale, the price difference with nonorganic foods may decrease.

Staying Informed

The world of food safety is fast paced and ever changing. Fortunately, the electronic age makes it much easier to access late-breaking information about newly recognized chemicals or pathogens that threaten public health. The public can be quickly informed of outbreaks or food recalls through various media sources. For those who need to keep up-to-date on food outbreaks, it is possible to subscribe to Web feeds or to install a food safety widget on one's Web page or social media site. Consumer groups maintain blogs with regular postings about food safety legislation and food recalls. Many mobile phone apps are available that provide information on the amount of pesticides in foods and restaurant safety records. They also can interpret food labels based on bar codes and provide guidelines on whether a leftover pizza is safe to eat.

Demanding Change

When people read Upton Sinclair's *The Jungle* back in 1906, they got mad. They got so mad that they let Congress know they wanted something done to clean up the meat industry. There followed the first real government action to regulate the quality of food sold in the United States. You probably think you have enough to worry about without keeping up with the latest food legislation in Washington, D.C., or in your state or city government. But every day, actions are being taken by elected officials, government employees, and industry lobbyists that will have a huge impact on the future of food safety.

Many of the actions that are intended to reduce hazards in our food and water may result in higher costs. The public must consider the trade-offs involved. A city may need to upgrade its water treatment plant, which may cause taxes to go up. If the school lunch program is underfunded, it may economize by purchasing manufactured beef patties that endanger children's health. More inspectors are required to check the safety of imported foods, but this means that the government will grow larger. Farmers need to follow the rules for pesticides, but a farm family may lose income as a result.

On the other side of the cost equation are the billions of dollars in expenses that result from foodborne illnesses each year.

In addition to medical costs for those requiring hospitalization, there are the costs of missing school or work that result from less serious cases of foodborne illness. For the unlucky few left with long-term disabilities, the dollar and emotional costs are very high.

Marion Nestle is a professor at New York University and an expert on food policy. In her opinion, today's consumers should demand the following: science-based food regulations, a single food agency to enforce regulations, a ban on nontherapeutic antibiotics in livestock, educational campaigns on the importance of hand-washing (including restaurant personnel), and campaign finance reform that would allow legislators to focus on public health rather than corporate health. Just like the people who were angered by what they learned from Sinclair's novel, *The Jungle*, today's informed public can change policies by letting their elected officials know of their concerns.

REVIEW

Although the food supply is for the most part safe and wholesome, most food experts agree that more must be done in order to reduce the burden of foodborne illnesses. Science-based decisions regarding food safety often come in conflict with public perceptions or political realities. Future improvements may include the irradiation of certain food products, the raising of livestock that are less likely to harbor human pathogens, and the use of genetic methods to track down disease sources or improve food crops. Consumers can play an important role in preventing foodborne illness by informing themselves about risks, choosing foods less likely to be contaminated, and following recommended food-handling procedures. Consumers can also influence the future of food safety by letting their elected officials know that they support efforts to extend and modernize current regulations.

APPENDIX A

DIETARY REFERENCE INTAKES

ACCEPTABLE MACRONUTRIENT DISTRIBUTION RANGES (AMDR) FOR HEALTHY DIETS AS A PERCENTAGE OF ENERGY

Age	Carbohydrates	Added Sugars	Total Fat	Linoleic Acid	α-Linolenic Acid	Protein
1–3 years old	45–65	25	30–40	5–10	0.6–1.2	5–20
4–18 years old	45–65	25	25–35	5–10	0.6–1.2	10–30
≥ 19 years old	45–65	25	20–35	5–10	0.6–1.2	10–35

Source: Institute of Medicine, Food and Nutrition Board. "Dietary Reference Intakes for Energy, Carbohydrates, Fiber, Fat, Protein, and Amino Acids." Washington, D.C.: National Academies Press, 2002.

RECOMMENDED INTAKES OF VITAMINS FOR VARIOUS AGE GROUPS

Life Stage	Vit A (μg/day)	Vit C (mg/day)	Vit D (μg/day)	Vit E (mg/day)	Vit K (μg/day)
Infants					
0–6 mo	400	40	5	4	2.0
7–12 mo	500	50	5	5	2.5
Children					
1–3 yrs	**300**	**15**	5	**6**	30
4–8 yrs	**400**	**25**	5	**7**	55
Males					
9–13 yrs	**600**	**45**	5	**11**	60
14–18 yrs	**900**	**75**	5	**15**	75
19–30 yrs	**900**	**90**	5	**15**	120
31–50 yrs	**900**	**90**	5	**15**	120
51–70 yrs	**900**	**90**	10	**15**	120
>70 yrs	**900**	**90**	15	**15**	120
Females					
9–13 yrs	**600**	**45**	5	**11**	60
14–18 yrs	**700**	**65**	5	**15**	75
19–30 yrs	**700**	**75**	5	**15**	90
31–50 yrs	**700**	**75**	5	**15**	90
51–70 yrs	**700**	**75**	10	**15**	90
>70 yrs	**700**	**75**	15	**15**	90
Pregnancy					
≤18 yrs	**750**	**80**	5	**15**	75
19–30 yrs	**770**	**85**	5	**15**	90
31–50 yrs	**770**	**85**	5	**15**	90
Lactation					
≤18 yrs	**1,200**	**115**	5	**19**	75
19–30 yrs	**1,300**	**120**	5	**19**	90
31–50 yrs	**1,300**	**120**	5	**19**	90

(continues)

RECOMMENDED INTAKES OF VITAMINS
FOR VARIOUS AGE GROUPS (continued)

Life Stage	Thiamin (mg/day)	Riboflavin (mg/day)	Niacin (mg/day)	Vit B$_6$ (mg/day)	Folate (µg/day)
Infants					
0–6 mo	0.2	0.3	2	0.1	65
7–12 mo	0.3	0.4	4	0.3	80
Children					
1–3 yrs	0.5	0.5	6	0.5	150
4–8 yrs	0.6	0.6	8	0.6	200
Males					
9–13 yrs	0.9	0.9	12	1.0	300
14–18 yrs	1.2	1.3	16	1.3	400
19–30 yrs	1.2	1.3	16	1.3	400
31–50 yrs	1.2	1.3	16	1.3	400
51–70 yrs	1.2	1.3	16	1.7	400
>70 yrs	1.2	1.3	16	1.7	400
Females					
9–13 yrs	0.9	0.9	12	1.0	300
14–18 yrs	1.0	1.0	14	1.2	400
19–30 yrs	1.1	1.1	14	1.3	400
31–50 yrs	1.1	1.1	14	1.3	400
51–70 yrs	1.1	1.1	14	1.5	400
>70 yrs	1.1	1.1	14	1.5	400
Pregnancy					
≤18 yrs	1.4	1.4	18	1.9	600
19–30 yrs	1.4	1.4	18	1.9	600
31–50 yrs	1.4	1.4	18	1.9	600
Lactation					
≤18 yrs	1.4	1.6	17	2.0	500
19–30 yrs	1.4	1.6	17	2.0	500
31–50 yrs	1.4	1.6	17	2.0	500

RECOMMENDED INTAKES OF VITAMINS FOR VARIOUS AGE GROUPS

Life Stage	Vit B$_{12}$ (µg/day)	Pantothenic Acid (mg/day)	Biotin Group (µg/day)	Choline* (mg/day)
Infants				
0–6 mo	0.4	1.7	5	125
7–12 mo	0.5	1.8	6	150
Children				
1–3 yrs	0.9	2	8	200
4–8 yrs	1.2	3	12	250
Males				
9–13 yrs	1.8	4	20	375
14–18 yrs	2.4	5	25	550
19–30 yrs	2.4	5	30	550
31–50 yrs	2.4	5	30	550
51–70 yrs	2.4	5	30	550
>70 yrs	2.4	5	30	550
Females				
9–13 yrs	1.8	4	20	375
14–18 yrs	2.4	5	25	400
19–30 yrs	2.4	5	30	425
31–50 yrs	2.4	5	30	425
51–70 yrs	2.4	5	30	425
>70 yrs	2.4	5	30	425
Pregnancy				
≤18 yrs	2.6	6	30	450
19–30 yrs	2.6	6	30	450
31–50 yrs	2.6	6	30	450
Lactation				
≤18 yrs	2.8	7	35	550
19–30 yrs	2.8	7	35	550
31–50 yrs	2.8	7	35	550

Note: This table presents Recommended Dietary Allowances (RDAs) in bold type and Adequate Intakes (AIs) in ordinary type.

* Not yet classified as a vitamin

Source: Adapted from Dietary Reference Intake Tables: The Complete Set. Institute of Medicine, National Academy of Sciences. Available online at www.nap.edu.

RECOMMENDED INTAKES OF SELECTED MINERALS FOR VARIOUS AGE GROUPS

Life Stage	Calcium (mg/day)	Chromium (µg/day)	Copper (µg/day)	Fluroide (mg/day)	Iodine (µg/day)
Infants					
0–6 mo	210	0.2	200	0.01	110
7–12 mo	270	5.5	220	0.5	130
Children					
1–3 yrs	500	11	340	0.7	90
4–8 yrs	800	15	440	1	90
Males					
9–13 yrs	1,300	25	700	2	120
14–18 yrs	1,300	35	890	3	150
19–30 yrs	1,000	35	900	4	150
31–50 yrs	1,000	35	900	4	150
51–70 yrs	1,200	30	900	4	150
>70 yrs	1,200	30	900	4	150
Females					
9–13 yrs	1,300	21	700	2	120
14–18 yrs	1,300	24	890	3	150
19–30 yrs	1,000	25	900	3	150
31–50 yrs	1,000	25	900	3	150
51–70 yrs	1,200	20	900	3	150
>70 yrs	1,200	20	900	3	150
Pregnancy					
≤18 yrs	1,300	29	1,000	3	220
19–30 yrs	1,000	30	1,000	3	220
31–50 yrs	1,000	30	1,000	3	220
Lactation					
≤18 yrs	1,300	44	1,300	3	290
19–30 yrs	1,000	45	1,300	3	290
31–50 yrs	1,000	45	1,300	3	290

RECOMMENDED INTAKES OF SELECTED MINERALS FOR VARIOUS AGE GROUPS

Life Stage	Iron (mg/day)	Magnesium (mg/day)	Phosphorus (mg/day)	Selenium (µg/day)
Infants				
0–6 mo	0.27	30	100	15
7–12 mo	11	75	275	20
Children				
1–3 yrs	7	80	460	20
4–8 yrs	10	130	500	30
Males				
9–13 yrs	8	240	1,250	40
14–18 yrs	11	410	1,250	55
19–30 yrs	8	400	700	55
31–50 yrs	8	420	700	55
51–70 yrs	8	420	700	55
>70 yrs	8	420	700	55
Females				
9–13 yrs	8	240	1,250	40
14–18 yrs	15	360	1,250	55
19–30 yrs	18	310	700	55
31–50 yrs	18	320	700	55
51–70 yrs	8	320	700	55
>70 yrs	8	320	700	55
Pregnancy				
≤18 yrs	27	400	1,250	60
19–30 yrs	27	350	700	60
31–50 yrs	27	360	700	60
Lactation				
≤18 yrs	10	360	1,250	70
19–30 yrs	9	310	700	70
31–50 yrs	9	320	700	70

(continues)

RECOMMENDED INTAKES OF SELECTED
MINERALS FOR VARIOUS AGE GROUPS (continued)

Life Stage	Zinc (mg/day)	Sodium (g/day)	Chloride (g/day)	Potassium (g/day)
Infants				
0–6 mo	2	0.12	0.18	0.4
7–12 mo	3	0.37	0.57	0.7
Children				
1–3 yrs	3	1.0	1.5	3.0
4–8 yrs	5	1.2	1.9	3.8
Males				
9–13 yrs	8	1.5	2.3	4.5
14–18 yrs	11	1.5	2.3	4.7
19–30 yrs	11	1.5	2.3	4.7
31–50 yrs	11	1.5	2.3	4.7
51–70 yrs	11	1.3	2.0	4.7
>70 yrs	11	1.2	1.8	4.7
Females				
9–13 yrs	8	1.5	2.3	4.5
14–18 yrs	9	1.5	2.3	4.7
19–30 yrs	8	1.5	2.3	4.7
31–50 yrs	8	1.5	2.3	4.7
51–70 yrs	8	1.3	2.0	4.7
>70 yrs	8	1.2	1.8	4.7
Pregnancy				
≤18 yrs	13	1.5	2.3	4.7
19–30 yrs	11	1.5	2.3	4.7
31–50 yrs	11	1.5	2.3	4.7
Lactation				
≤18 yrs	14	1.5	2.3	5.1
19–30 yrs	12	1.5	2.3	5.1
31–50 yrs	12	1.5	2.3	5.1

Note: This table presents Recommended Dietary Allowances (RDAs) in bold type and Adequate Intakes (AIs) in ordinary type.

Source: Adapted from Dietary Reference Intake Tables: The Complete Set. Institute of Medicine, National Academy of Sciences. Available online at www.nap.edu.

APPENDIX B

HEALTHY BODY WEIGHTS
Body Mass Index (BMI)

Body mass index, or BMI, is the measurement of choice for determining health risks associated with body weight. BMI uses a mathematical formula that takes into account both a person's height and weight. BMI equals a person's weight in kilograms divided by height in meters squared ($BMI = kg/m^2$).

RISK OF ASSOCIATED DISEASE ACCORDING TO BMI AND WAIST SIZE FOR ADULTS

BMI		Waist less than or equal to 40 in. (men) or 35 in. (women)	Waist greater than 40 in. (men) or 35 in. (women)
18.5 or less	Underweight	N/A	N/A
18.5–24.9	Normal	N/A	N/A
25.0–29.9	Overweight	Increased	High
30.0–34.9	Obese	High	Very High
35.0–39.9	Obese	Very High	Very High
40 or greater	Extremely Obese	Extremely High	Extremely High

Determining Your Body Mass Index (BMI)

To use the table on the following page, find the appropriate height in the left-hand column. Move across the row to the given weight. The number at the top of the column is the BMI for that height and weight. Then use the table above to determine how at risk you are for developing a weight-related disease.

157

BMI (kg/m²)	19	20	21	22	23	24	25	26	27	28	29	30	35	40
Height (in.)	Weight (lb)													
58	91	96	100	105	110	115	119	124	129	134	138	143	167	191
59	94	99	104	109	114	119	124	128	133	138	143	148	173	198
60	97	102	107	112	118	123	128	133	138	143	148	153	179	204
61	100	106	111	116	122	127	132	137	143	148	153	158	185	211
62	104	109	115	120	126	131	136	142	147	153	158	164	191	218
63	107	113	118	124	130	135	141	146	152	158	163	169	197	225
64	110	116	122	128	134	140	145	151	157	163	169	174	204	232
65	114	120	126	132	138	144	150	156	162	168	174	180	210	240
66	118	124	130	136	142	148	155	161	167	173	179	186	216	247
67	121	127	134	140	146	153	159	166	172	178	185	191	223	255
68	125	131	138	144	151	158	164	171	177	184	190	197	230	262
69	128	135	142	149	155	162	169	176	182	189	196	203	236	270
70	132	139	146	153	160	167	174	181	188	195	202	207	243	278
71	136	143	150	157	165	172	179	186	193	200	208	215	250	286
72	140	147	154	162	169	177	184	191	199	206	213	221	258	294
73	144	151	159	166	174	182	189	197	204	212	219	227	265	302
74	148	155	163	171	179	186	194	202	210	218	225	233	272	311
75	152	160	168	176	184	192	200	208	216	224	232	240	279	319
76	156	164	172	180	189	197	205	213	221	230	238	246	287	328

Source: Adapted from Partnership for Healthy Weight Management, http://www.consumer.gov/weightloss/bmi.htm.

BMI-FOR-AGE GROWTH CHARTS

2 to 20 years: Boys
Body mass index-for-age percentiles

NAME

RECORD #

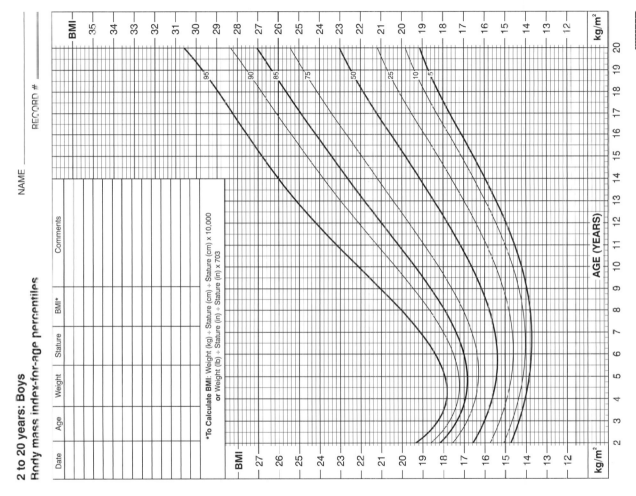

Date	Age	Weight	Stature	BMI*	Comments

*To Calculate BMI: Weight (kg) ÷ Stature (cm) ÷ Stature (cm) x 10,000
or Weight (lb) ÷ Stature (in) ÷ Stature (in) x 703

AGE (YEARS)

Published May 30, 2000 (modified 10/16/00).
SOURCE: Developed by the National Center for Health Statistics in collaboration with
the National Center for Chronic Disease Prevention and Health Promotion (2000).
http://www.cdc.gov/growthcharts

SAFER · HEALTHIER · PEOPLE™

NAME _____

RECORD # _____

2 to 20 years: Girls
Body mass index-for-age percentiles

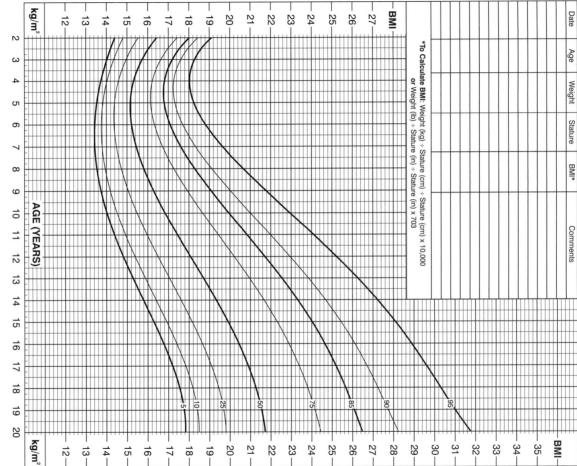

*To Calculate BMI: Weight (kg) ÷ Stature (cm) ÷ Stature (cm) x 10,000
or Weight (lb) ÷ Stature (in) ÷ Stature (in) x 703

Date	Age	Weight	Stature	BMI*	Comments

BMI

kg/m²

27
26
25
24
23
22
21
20
19
18
17
16
15
14
13
12

AGE (YEARS)

2 3 4 5 6 7 8 9 10 11 12 13 14 15 16 17 18 19 20

5 10 25 50 75 85 90 95

BMI

kg/m²

35
34
33
32
31
30
29
28
27
26
25
24
23
22
21
20
19
18
17
16
15
14
13
12

NUTRITION AND FOOD SAFETY

RECORD #

BMI

Published May 30, 2000 (modified 10/16/00).
SOURCE: Developed by the National Center for Health Statistics in collaboration with
the National Center for Chronic Disease Prevention and Health Promotion (2000).
http://www.cdc.gov/growthcharts

SAFER · HEALTHIER · PEOPLE™

APPENDIX C

BLOOD VALUES OF NUTRITIONAL RELEVANCE

Red blood cells	
Men	4.6–6.2 million/mm^3
Women	4.2–5.2 million/mm^3
White blood cells	5,000–10,000/mm^3
Calcium	9–11 mg/100 mL
Iron	
Men	75–175 μg/100 mL
Women	65–165 μg/100 mL
Zinc	0.75–1.4 μg/mL
Potassium	3.5–5.0 mEq/L
Sodium	136–145 mEq/L
Vitamin A	20–80 μg/100 mL
Vitamin B$_{12}$	200–800 pg/100 mL
Vitamin C	0.6–2.0 mg/100 mL
Folate	2–20 ng/mL
pH	7.35–7.45
Total protein	6.6–8.0 g/100 mL
Albumin	3.0–4.0 g/100 mL
Cholesterol	less than 200 mg/100 mL
Glucose	60–100 mg/100 mL blood, 70–120 mg/100 mL serum

Source: Handbook of Clinical Dietetics, *American Dietetic Association (New Haven, Conn.: Yale University Press, 1981); and Committee on Dietetics of the Mayo Clinic,* Mayo Clinic Diet Manual *(Philadelphia: W. B. Saunders Company, 1981), pp. 275–277.*

Anatomy of MyPyramid

One size doesn't fit all

USDA's new MyPyramid symbolizes a personalized approach to healthy eating and physical activity. The symbol has been designed to be simple. It has been developed to remind consumers to make healthy food choices and to be active every day. The different parts of the symbol are described below.

Activity

Activity is represented by the steps and the person climbing them, as a reminder of the importance of daily physical activity.

Moderation

Moderation is represented by the narrowing of each food group from bottom to top. The wider base stands for foods with little or no solid fats or added sugars. These should be selected more often. The narrower top area stands for foods containing more added sugars and solid fats. The more active you are, the more of these foods can fit into your diet.

Personalization

Personalization is shown by the person on the steps, the slogan, and the URL. Find the kinds and amounts of food to eat each day at MyPyramid.gov.

Proportionality

Proportionality is shown by the different widths of the food group bands. The widths suggest how much food a person should choose from each group. The widths are just a general guide, not exact proportions. Check the Web site for how much is right for you.

Variety

Variety is symbolized by the 6 color bands representing the 5 food groups of the Pyramid and oils. This illustrates that foods from all groups are needed each day for good health.

Gradual Improvement

Gradual improvement is encouraged by the slogan. It suggests that individuals can benefit from taking small steps to improve their diet and lifestyle each day.

MyPyramid.gov
STEPS TO A HEALTHIER YOU

U.S. Department of Agriculture
Center for Nutrition Policy
and Promotion
April 2005 CNPP-16

USDA is an equal opportunity provider and employer.

GRAINS	VEGETABLES	FRUITS	OILS	MILK	MEAT & BEANS

Source: http://www.mypyramid.gov/downloads/MyPyramid_Anatomy.pdf.

GLOSSARY

Adulteration Intentional addition of an inferior or undesirable substance to a food product, often for the purpose of lowering its cost

Allergen Normally harmless substance that triggers an immune response in a person with allergies; food allergens are proteins found in common foods such as eggs and nuts.

Anaphylaxis A possibly life-threatening allergic response, characterized by swelling around the eyes and mouth, and difficulty with swallowing and breathing

Antibiotic Drug used to treat bacterial infections; healthy livestock animals sometimes receive antibiotic treatment in order to prevent infections.

Antibody Protein produced by the body's immune system to protect against foreign substances

Bioterrorism Terrorism using a biological agent, such as a food or water pathogen

Bisphenol A (BPA) Chemical used in the production of hard plastics and epoxy resins; may occur in food by leaching from plastic bottles or can liners

Carrier A person who has no symptoms of disease but whose body harbors disease organisms; this person can spread the disease to other people.

Chromosome Structure within a cell that contains genetic material in the form of long strands of DNA

Clone A genetically identical copy of an organism

Contamination Unintended presence of harmful substance or microorganisms in food

Cross-contamination Transfer of bacteria or allergens from one food substance to another

Deoxyribonucleic acid (DNA)   Complex, helix-shaped chemical found in all cells that contains the organism's genetic code

DNA fingerprint   Pattern of DNA chemical structure, useful in matching specimens from outbreaks of foodborne illness

Epidemiology   Study of the causes, distribution, and control of diseases in a population

Feces   Waste matter eliminated from the intestinal tract; bowel movement

Food additive   Substance added to food during processing for purpose of preservation, taste, or color

Gastroenteritis   Inflammation of the stomach and intestines

Gene   Physical unit of inheritance consisting of a short sequence on a DNA molecule; a gene (or genes) may carry instructions for a particular trait, such as plant height.

Generally Recognized as Safe (GRAS)   An FDA designation indicating that qualified experts regard a substance to be a safe food; substances in this category are not subject to regulation as food additives.

Hazard Analysis Critical Control Point (HACCP)   A science-based method for control of food processing in order to eliminate pathogens

Heterocyclic amine (HCA)   Chemical formed when meats are cooked at high temperatures

Hormones   Chemicals that circulate in the bloodstream and control the action of cells and organs

Microorganisms   General term for bacteria, fungi, or viruses that can only be seen with a microscope

O157:H7   A virulent type of *E. coli* bacteria capable of causing foodborne illness

Outbreak   Occurrence of illness in a group of people after they have eaten food from the same contaminated food source

Pathogen   Organism capable of causing infection

Pesticide   Substance intended to repel or destroy pests; pests may be in the form of weeds, insects, or other organisms.

Quarantine   Confinement of a person with a contagious disease in order to prevent disease transmission

Recombinant bovine growth hormone (rBGH)   Genetically engineered growth hormone injected into dairy cattle for the purpose of increasing milk production

Recombinant DNA technology   Insertion of the DNA for a desirable gene from one organism permanently into the DNA of another organism

Residue   Small amount of a chemical, such as a pesticide, that remains on or in a food product

Slaughterhouse   Building where animals are killed and butchered for food

Tolerance level   Amount of a contaminant, such as a pesticide, that a food is allowed to contain by law

Toxin   A poisonous substance produced by living cells or organisms

Blatt, Harvey. *America's Food: What You Don't Know about What You Eat*. Cambridge, Mass.: The MIT Press, 2008.

Center for Science in the Public Interest. *Makers of Quorn®, the Chicken-Flavored Fungus, Sued for Not Disclosing Dangerous Reactions*. Available at: http://www.cspinet.org/new/20090171.html. Accessed February 15, 2010.

Dawson, Paul A., I. Han, M. Cox, C. Black, and L. Simmons. "Residence Time and Food Contact Time Effects on Transfer of *Salmonella Typhimurium* from Tile, Wood, and Carpet: Testing the Five-Second Rule." *Journal of Applied Microbiology* 102 (2007): 945–953.

Duhigg, Charles. "Millions in U.S. Drink Dirty Water, Records Say." *The New York Times*, December 8, 2009, A1, A3.

———. "That Tap Water Is Legal but May Be Unhealthy." *The New York Times*, December 17, 2009, A1, A30-A31.

Food and Drug Administration. *Bad Bug Book*. Available at: http://www.fda.gov/Food/FoodSafety/FoodborneIllness/Foodborne IllnessFoodbornePathogensNaturalToxins/BadBugBook/default. htm Accessed February 10, 2010.

Hardnett, F.P., R.M. Hoekstra, M. Kennedy, L. Charles, F.J. Angulo, "Epidemiologic Issues in Study Design and Data Analysis Related to FoodNet Activities." *Clinical Infectious Diseases* 39, Suppl. 3 (2004): 121-126.

Homeland Security Newswire. *25 Years to Oregon Salmonella Terrorism*. Available at: http://homelandsecuritynewswire.com/25-years-oregon-salmonella-bioterrorism. Accessed February 21, 2010.

Human Genome Project. "Genetically Modified Foods and Organisms." Available at: http://www.ornl.gov/sci/techresources/Human_ Genome/elsi/gmfood.shtml. Accessed February 11, 2010.

Jacobson, Michael and Bruce Silverglade. "What the Label Doesn't Tell You." *Nutrition Action Healthletter* (December 2009).

Johnson, Steven. *The Ghost Map: The Story of London's Most Terrifying Epidemic—and How It Changed Science, Cities, and the Modern World.* New York: Penguin Group, 2006.

Joneja, Janice V. *Dealing with Food Allergies in Babies and Children.* Boulder, Colo.: Bull Publishing Co., 2007.

Kristof, Nicholas D. "Something Scary in the Pantry." *The New York Times,* November 8, 2009, WK10.

Lienhard, John H. "Bosch's Demons." *Engines of Our Ingenuity.* Available at: http://www.uh.edu/engines/epi258.htm. Accessed February 15, 2010.

McGee, Harold. "The Five-Second Rule Explored, or How Dirty Is That Bologna." *The New York Times,* May 9, 2007, F3.

Moss, Michael. "The Burger That Shattered Her Life." *The New York Times,* October 4, 2009, 1, 24–25.

National Cancer Institute Fact Sheet: Heterocyclic Amines in Cooked Meats. Available at: http://www.cancer.gov/cancertopics/factsheet/Risk/heterocyclic-amines. Accessed February 15, 2010.

National Toxicology Program Fact Sheet: Bisphenol A (BPA). Available at: http://www.niehs.nih.gov/health/docs/bpa-factsheet.pdf. Accessed February 15, 2010.

Nestle, Marion. *Safe Food: Bacteria, Biotechnology, and Bioterrorism.* Berkeley: University of California Press, 2003.

Nestle, Marion. *What to Eat.* New York: North Point Press, 2006.

Neuman, William. "After Delays, Vaccine Is Tested in Fight Against Tainted Beef." *The New York Times,* December 4, 2009, A1, A25.

Rice, Marlin. "Monarchs and Bt Corn: A Research Update." *Integrated Crop Management* 488 (2002): 13–14.

Ronald, Pamela C. and Raoul W. Adamchak. *Tomorrow's Table: Organic Farming, Genetics, and the Future of Food.* New York: Oxford University Press, 2008.

Satin, Morton. *Death in the Pot: The Impact of Food Poisoning on History.* Amherst, N.Y.: Prometheus Books, 2007.

Sinclair, Upton. *The Jungle* (Penguin Classics). New York: Penguin Group, 2006.

Sperber, William H. and Richard F. Stier. "Happy 50th Birthday to HACCP: Retrospective and Prospective." *Food Safety Magazine,* (Dec. 2009/Jan. 2010).

Tucker, Jonathan B. *Historical Trends Related to Bioterrorism: An Empirical Analysis.* Available at: http://cdc.gov/ncidod/EID/vol5no4/tucker.htm. Accessed February 15, 2010.

University of California-San Francisco. "Iodine Allergy and Contrast Administration." Available at: http://www.radiology.ucsf.edu/patients/iodine_allergy. Accessed January 28, 2010.

Vileisis, Ann. *Kitchen Literacy: How We Lost Knowledge of Where Food Comes from and Why We Need to Get It Back.* Washington, D.C.: Island Press, 2008.

Walters Mark J. *Six Modern Plagues and How We Are Causing Them.* Washington, D.C.: Island Press, 2003.

Weber, Karl (ed.). *Food, Inc.: How Industrial Food Is Making Us Sicker, Fatter and Poorer—And What You Can Do about It.* New York: PublicAffairs, 2009.

Wilson, Bee. *Swindled: The Dark History of Food Fraud, from Poisoned Candy to Counterfeit Coffee.* Princeton, N.J.: Princeton University Press, 2008.

FURTHER RESOURCES

Herbst, Judith. *Germ Theory*. Minneapolis, Minn: Twenty-First Century Books, 2008.

Klein, Sarah and Caroline Smith DeWall. "Dirty Dining." Washington, D.C. Center for Science in the Public Interest, 2008. Available at: http://cspinet.org/dirtydining/index.html.

Lennard-Brown, Sarah. *Allergies*. Chicago: Raintree, 2004.

Leon, Warren and Caroline Smith DeWaal. *Is Your Food Safe? A Consumer's Guide to Protecting Your Health and the Environment*. New York: Three Rivers Press, 2002.

Pringle, Peter. *Food, Inc.: Mendel to Monsanto: The Promises and Perils of the Biotech Harvest*. New York: Simon & Schuster, 2003.

Smith, Terry L. *Modern Genetic Science: New Technology, New Decisions*. New York. The Rosen Publishing Group, 2009.

WEB SITES

Center for Foodborne Illness Research and Prevention
http://www.foodborneillness.org/
The site includes information on science-based solutions for preventing foodborne illnesses.

Environmental Protection Agency (EPA)
http://www.epa.gov/highschool/
This site includes information from the EPA about pesticides, mercury, water pollution, and other issues.

Federal Food Safety Information
http://foodsafety.gov/
This comprehensive food safety Web site includes current information about outbreaks, descriptions of common foodborne illnesses, and consumer guides for keeping food safe.

Food and Drug Administration (FDA)

http://www.fda.gov/

This site provides information on wide range of food topics, such as ingredients, packaging, labeling, defense, and FDA news releases.

Kids Health

http://kidshealth.org/teen/

Learn how to buy, prepare, and store food to avoid foodborne illnesses.

U.S. Department of Agriculture (USDA)

http://www.usda.gov/

The site offers information about USDA programs, consumer food safety information, organic certification, and news releases.

PICTURE CREDITS

Page numbers in *italics* indicate photos or illustrations.

ABOUT THE AUTHOR

TERRY L. SMITH is a biostatistician and science writer who lives in Lawrence, Kansas. She has an M.S. in biometry from the University of Texas School of Public Health. Smith is the author of numerous books and articles relating to human health, including *Asthma* in Chelsea House's **GENES AND DISEASE** series.